PAY CHECKS AND PLAY CHECKS

RETIREMENT SOLUTIONS FOR LIFE

TOM HEGNA

Printed in the United States of America
ISBN: 978-0-9842173-8-0

Published by Acanthus Publishing, Boston, Massachusetts.

Cover images: © iStockphoto.com/spxChrome, iStockphoto.com/alexsl

Table of Contents

Preface

In recent years, it seems as though the media have focused almost exclusively on the world's hardships – recessions, financial collapse, war, civil unrest, and so on. The truth is that we have faced such tumultuous times for centuries. Read the history books as far back as you please; they will all document the consistency of world change and troubled times. I don't know. For me, it just feels different this time. The range of possible outcomes for our economy, our way of life, and our country as a whole is the widest I can remember during my lifetime. In the current financial environment, with all of the government intervention and printing of money, we do not even know what is real or what information we can depend on. We could soon see deflation, or we could just as easily see hyperinflation. The economy could continue its pattern of slow recovery, but it could also very well plummet into the next Great Depression. These are truly not normal times.

One drastic consequence of this financial downturn is that traditional safety nets such as pensions and Social Security are rapidly disappearing. This situation, of course, happens to coincide with the retirement of over 78 million baby boomers who crave the same lifetime benefits their parents had. The first group of boomers will turn 65 in 2011. I am a baby boomer too, and thus felt compelled to write this book as a necessary roadmap for those who want to retire successfully and comfortably. My book is not based on my opinions. It is the product of careful research. I have been speaking around the world on the topic of retirement planning for over a decade, and this book will share with you the best strategies I have been able to discover for planning your golden years.

I am fascinated by how excited people get when they find that a successful retirement is possible. They can have a retirement that is not only successful, but also worry-free; a retirement with the financial flexibility to handle unforeseen events and face unexpected economic times triggered by inflation, deflation, and stock market and real estate booms and busts. Regardless of the economy's present or future state, those who read this book will learn to retire with minimal risk and maximum satisfaction. Some people think this scenario is too good to be true. Others are skeptical. Here is what I say: The research is clear. There is one optimal way to retire. This book will lay out the math and science behind having a successful and stress-free retirement.

The front page article of the April 4, 2011 *Wall Street Journal* was the tipping point for me to begin writing this book. The headline read, "Fed's Low Interest Rates Crack Retiree's Nest Eggs." The article focused on a gentleman by the name of Forrest Yeager, a 91-year-old resident of Port Charlotte,

Florida. With his Certificates of Deposit paying less than 1%, his remaining $45,000 of retirement savings was providing just a few hundred dollars per year – forcing him to withdraw principal to live his current lifestyle. He believes his money will run out before he dies. Other retirees mentioned in the article had moved their money to stocks or high-yield bonds, subjecting their only savings to significant risk while losing their peace of mind.

That was it for me. I realized I had to get the word out. You do not have to live like that! You do not have to settle for 1% CD's – in fact, you absolutely should not. Mr. Yeager could walk into almost any reputable insurance company in America today and be guaranteed a payout of over 20% each year for the rest of his life! Think about that – in his case, $9,000 per year with zero market risk (I will explain this more in-depth in later chapters).

That same article went on to say, "The longer the central bank keeps interest rates low to stimulate the economy, the more money it pulls out of the pockets of millions of savers." These low interest rates are part of Federal Reserve Chairman Ben Bernanke's plan to help recapitalize the banks.

"Americans who have done everything right, have worked hard, saved their money and stayed out of debt are the ones being punished by low interest rates," says Richard Fisher, president of the Federal Reserve Bank of Dallas and a voting member of the Fed's policy-making open market committee. "That state of affairs is not sustainable for a long period of time."

Luckily, you do not have to put all of your retirement savings into the stock market or junk bonds – and again, you shouldn't. That, of course, does not mean you should not invest at least some of your money in stocks, bonds, real estate, or commodities. You should. But what is the right mix? If you ask 50 different financial advisors, you will get 50 different "opinions." Unfortunately, these opinions likely will be sub-optimal. Instead of offering you my opinion, I am going to lay out for you the math and science behind a very simple retirement solution. It is so simple, in fact, that you will probably ask yourself, "Why doesn't every financial advisor know this?"

So there you have it: I wrote this book to provide simple and effective financial strategies for upcoming retirees. After almost every seminar I gave over the last 15 years (and I have given somewhere near 3,000) someone would inevitably come up to me and say, "You should write a book. You make this sound so simple." Well, it is simple and I am a big believer in simplicity.

Whenever I offer advice on financial matters, I try to explain concepts as simply as possible. It is not that clients don't have the capacity to understand complex ideas, but most people just do not want or need their finances to be complicated. Besides, people rarely lose money in a simple product like a CD, fixed annuity, or money market fund. No, it is usually some complicated investment scheme that sounded great at the time but that the investor did not understand.

My last bit of advice before I begin: always do your homework. In the financial world, it is called due diligence. Research your broker or financial advisor. Call their references. Search for indicators of professionalism, ethics, and excellence. One good indicator is longevity (the longer someone has been in the business, the less likely they are doing something wrong or illegal). I always say, "Time is the friend of those who do business the right way, and it's the enemy of those who don't." Look for professional designations (the letters after their name) – again, no guarantee that the person is not a crook but it establishes some level of training, ethics, and professionalism. Look at the company they have aligned themselves with. Is it a reputable company? Can you do research on their recommendations? Will they cite their references for their recommendations? I want you to do your due diligence on my recommendations as well. That way, you will be fully confident and committed to a successful retirement.

So for Mr. Yeager and the millions of retirees just like him, this book is for you.

Chapter 1

What Happened to Happily Ever After?

As Bob Dylan once sang, the times they are a-changin'. Believe it or not, there was a time in this country when you could retire gracefully and worry-free. Your employer held a little going away party, presented you a shiny gold watch, and gave you a guaranteed paycheck for life in the form of a nice pension to keep you comfortable and allow you to live happily ever after – just like the fairy tales of old.

This, unfortunately, is no longer the case. It is more than likely that upon retiring, you will not receive a pension. Like dinosaurs, these plans have been going extinct ever since companies realized it was cheaper to match employee contributions to a 401(k) plan. The extinction of these plans has been hastened by a number of alarming defaults, highlighting the dangers and pitfalls of the pension system.

So what is left for you? Your 401(k)? Unless you have been hiding under a rock for the past few years, you know what happened in 2008. The financial system crashed. Stock prices plummeted. You are probably left with two-thirds (or less!) of what you had hoped to save just five years ago. With inflation and a volatile market ahead, savings alone might not be enough to ensure you the retirement you deserve. Given that many of us will live about 25 years or more after retirement, there is a real possibility that you could deplete your savings – hardly my definition of "golden years."

And what about Social Security? The monthly check seniors could once depend on is about to get a whole lot less dependable. Considering the nation's enormous government deficits and the current demand to keep taxes low, Social Security is not a self-sustaining enterprise. You may be able to count on a check; but will it be enough?

The balance of this chapter will examine today's problems with retirement – and find tomorrow's solutions using hard evidence. I do not like opinions; I like facts. Mathematic, scientific, and economic facts. I am going to lay the facts out in front of you and help you decide the best course of action.

Pension Problems

Pensions used to form the third leg of the retirement planning stool along with Social Security and savings. Pensions are great – who wouldn't want guaranteed income for life? It is just that pensions do not really exist anymore for most retirees.

In your father's day, workers could count on receiving a lifelong check from their former employers. For most companies, this simply is not economically feasible anymore. Given that retirees are living longer and U.S. companies face stiff competition in the global economy, 401(k) plans became a better deal as businesses sought to boost profits and limit liabilities. Today, only about 19% of our workforce can claim a pension after retirement, and most of those jobs fall under the government sector. And if you have been paying attention to the news, even government pensions are diminishing as state budgets have been strapped for revenue, leaving state pensions with a potential shortfall of over $3 trillion. In the private sector, pension funds for the companies in the S&P 500 were underfunded to the tune of $245 billion at the end of 2010.

Most companies are watching their pension costs go through the roof because they failed to set aside enough money to fund the benefits and retirees are living longer. The plans also promised payments that were just too high based on current life expectancy. Additionally, due to market volatility and poor stock market returns over the past decade, the investments backing the pensions have underperformed. It therefore comes as no surprise that big corporations such as IBM have completely frozen their pension plans over the past few years and shifted to a 401(k) plan. The trend in companies has been to start contributing to 401(k)s instead of traditional pension plans, which shifts more of the risks to the individual worker. To further complicate matters, other large companies, including FedEx, General Motors, and Eastman Kodak, have suspended matching contributions to their employees' 401(k) plans in recent years. Many companies have restored their matching contributions with the end of the financial panic, but often at a reduced level. So even the less costly 401(k) retirement plan is not holding up, let alone the dying pension system.

When a pension plan goes belly up, the company transfers its pension problems onto the government, which runs a program called the Pension Benefit Guarantee Corporation. The PBGC pays out about 80% of what retirees would have received otherwise. The payouts are also capped, which can devastate higher-income workers who were expecting larger pensions. I remember reading the horror stories of the retired airline pilots who only received a fraction of what they had been promised. Like most government institutions, the PBGC is in the red. All companies that offer pensions pay a premium to the PBGC. When a company defaults on a pension, the PBGC is pressured to raise premiums, which subsequently increases costs and pressures companies into getting rid of expensive programs – like pensions.

While I would like to say that only the most mismanaged companies default on pensions, that sadly is not the case. It does not always occur because of incompetent management; market innovations and competition play a key role as well. Take Polaroid, for instance. They were a huge enterprise with numerous product innovations through the years. Then, about 10 years ago, digital cameras started showing up. Sales slowed down. Now, Polaroid is gone, and so is their pension plan! A decade ago, few would have predicted this dramatic turn of events. The point is that you probably do not have a pension, and you might need to worry about a default if you do. It is an unfortunate fact that this is the case, because there really is nothing like a guaranteed lifetime income stream. In this book we will attempt to find a new one.

The Panic of 2008 and What it Means for Your 401(k)

You know what happened in 2008. If you have even glanced at a newspaper in the past three years, you know what happened. People invested in real estate because they thought the housing market was never, ever, going to crash. Well, guess what? It did.

The statistics say it all. Millions of lost jobs and trillions of government dollars going to troubled businesses, banks, and whoever else qualified for a handout. A 50% free fall for the Dow Jones. The last one hurt the most. Those who didn't know about the strategies I will share with you got hit pretty badly. A decade's worth of gains was wiped out. The era of steady double-digit returns was a distant memory.

Fast forward to 2014 – the markets have recovered from the 2008 crash. But guess what? Many people were not in the market to see the recovery. If you think about it, these people lost TWICE – once when the market crashed and again when the market recovered its losses but they had sold at the bottom! the This is still a whole new world for your retirement savings.

For one, individuals and institutions are not going to be as willing to invest their money in risky ventures like we saw in the subprime mess. On the bright side, we probably will not see another big stock market bubble or real estate bubble anytime soon. But you have to remember that over the long term, those who understand risk win. A market without much risk is a market without much opportunity.

There is another hidden aspect to this great recession. After we finally pull ourselves out of it, get back out there, and get paid, we may get hit with serious long-term inflation. The government printed a lot of extra cash to avoid the worst of the recession. Once the downturn is over, what happens? All those extra printed dollars are just going to be floating around, and it is going to cost more of them to get the same products. It is very easy for governments to print money, but it is much more difficult to pull it back out: doing so causes unemployment to rise and stocks to fall. For the long term, you have to keep inflation in mind.

These price-inflated products will include two resources retirees cannot go without: oil and food. Despite some fluctuation from shifts in both domestic and foreign markets, oil and food are steadily becoming more expensive. For example, according to the U.S. Energy Information Administration, crude oil prices, which hovered around $60 a barrel in 2006, shot up to over $100 a barrel by April 2011. This is inflation at its worst, nearly doubling the cost of oil in only five years. It permeates the economy from gas prices to the cost of shipping goods to market.

Food prices have also been rising. Take coffee for example. Folgers Coffee, the best-selling U.S. brand, announced an 11% price increase after the cost of beans almost doubled in the past year. Increased food costs are showing up everywhere from McDonald's to Whole Foods. Then there is the "stealth" food inflation – items ranging from canned tuna fish to potato chips are shrinking in portion size by 10-20%. The price may be the same, but you are getting less for your money.

Retirees are therefore facing a double whammy from low returns and higher prices. You cannot count on getting large returns for your money anymore. You probably can count on your diminished returns buying you less for your dollar.

The Social Security Dilemma

You have probably heard about some of the troubles with Social Security. There are 78 million baby boomers in America (about 26% of the population), and every last one of them is rushing headlong into retirement. One by one, each baby boomer will soon stop working, stop contributing to Social Security, and start taking money from the program. Payroll taxes are used to fund the program, with any surplus held in a trust fund to help cover the cost of the boomers' retirement. However, the trust fund is actually a pile of IOUs. Congress has already spent the money! Furthermore, the monthly benefit payments certainly will not be enough to cover average living expenses. The Social Security Administration reported that the average monthly benefit for senior and/or disabled citizens was $1,077 in 2011, and it is quite probable that the payment you receive in the future will be even less than this. But even assuming $1,000 monthly payments, $12,000 a year simply cannot cover all of a typical retiree's costs, and these circumstances are simply not going to improve.

At this time, the U.S. government does not foresee any significant increases in Social Security payments. Decreases, on the other hand, are more than possible. This is partly because the program covers far more people than just retirees and the disabled. It also provides other services such as unemployment benefits and children's health insurance. With all of these programs lumped together and supported by a practically empty fund, the future of the program appears grim.

For all its problems, Social Security was actually quite workable when it was first created back in the 1930s. The payments were sizable, and they kept a lot of older folks above the poverty line without breaking the government's credit. Here is the problem, though: during this era, there were far fewer beneficiaries compared with the number of workers paying into the system since people did not live as long as they do today. The average life expectancy in 1935, when the U.S. first established the Social Security Act, was age 60 for men and age 64 for women. It was fairly typical for

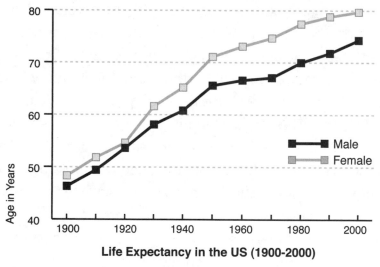

Life Expectancy in the US (1900-2000)

Data from: U.S. Congressional Research Service. Life Expectancy in the United States. (RL32792; Aug. 16, 2006), by Laura B. Shrestha.

Americans to pass away before they even reached age 65 and retired, leaving more Social Security money to the lucky few blessed with longevity. The situation is much different today, with people often living into their 80s or 90s.

Recent data indicates the average lifespan for women has gone from 71 years in 1960 to roughly 80 today and from 66 to 75 years for men. This means that Social Security will have to accommodate an unprecedented and overwhelming number of healthy, long-living retirees. Moreover, if you are married, you can count on an even longer average lifespan – by up to nine years.

Of course, increased life expectancy is not the only flaw in the Social Security system. Since the fund that is supposed to cover our checks in the future is merely a series of IOUs, the reserves are hardly liquid. Whenever the government needed to pay for something, it would take some cash out of the fund and leave an IOU. This short-term problem solver is now creating a huge headache, because unless that money is paid back, we are not going to have enough Social Security money to fund benefits at current levels.

Furthermore, the government will have raised the full retirement age from 65 to 67 before the year 2022. For those who opt to still retire at age 65, this will mean even lower monthly Social Security payments. On the flipside, those who remain working until age 67 will still miss out on two years of Social Security benefits that their parents received.

And as if that was not enough to prove my point, we also have to mix Medicare premiums and taxes into the equation. Medicare covers many healthcare expenses for seniors. However, some coverage is limited. For example, if you need long-term care, Medicare will only provide coverage for up to 100 days in a nursing home. Unfortunately, the program is also running low on money. You can probably guess what will happen over the next decade: Medicare Part B premiums deducted from Social Security benefits are projected to soar to over 10%, which will reduce the amount of your check. In addition, up to 85% of

Social Security benefits may be taxed for higher-income retirees. Since these taxes are not indexed for inflation, many middle-class earners will be viewed as "rich" and will have to pay higher taxes on their Social Security benefits.

So, what can you expect from Social Security in the future? Apparently not what your parents could. The past two years (2010 and 2011) have seen no increases in benefits. While cutting benefits or raising the age at which you could start collecting would have been political suicide just 10 years ago, the debt crisis has permanently changed things. No one can predict where Social Security benefits will be 10 years from now, but do not count on them being anywhere near as generous as they once were.

All this being said, I am not a Social Security doom-and-gloomer. I can confidently say that you *will* receive Social Security in retirement. The entire Social Security "problem" will not be that difficult to solve. It is a matter of understanding the economic realities and having the political will. In fact, two simple changes would fix the system for the rest of our lifetimes. First, gradually raising the retirement age by one month for every two years that you are younger than age 50. For instance, my dad got full Social Security at age 65; I won't get mine until age 67. Is it that unreasonable that my 9-year-old daughter won't get hers until 69 or 70? Her life expectancy will be longer than mine and my father's, after all.

The second change will have to come with the way Social Security benefits are initially calculated. Currently, the initial benefits for new retirees are increased each year based on wage growth (the rate of increase in the national average wage). However, if initial benefits were instead indexed to price growth (which measures actual purchasing power), the long-term solvency of the system would be ensured, according to a Social Security Administration report in 2010. The reason is that on average wages tend to grow faster than prices. As a result, price-indexed initial benefits would grow more slowly than wage-indexed initial benefits. The downside of indexing initial benefits to price growth is that it would mean slightly lower monthly benefit levels for future retirees than what they would have received under the current plan. Overall, though, Social Security will survive in some form. Future retirees might not get their parents' benefit amount in real (inflation-adjusted) terms, but they will receive a Social Security check in retirement and it will be greater in nominal dollars than what their parents received.

 Social Security – By the Numbers

Participants in 2011: 55 million
Spending in 2011: $733 billion
Projected participants in 2021: 72 million
Projected spending in 2021: $1.27 trillion
(Source: Congressional Budget Office)

 Medicare – By the Numbers

While Social Security might get fixed with a minor overhaul, I am not nearly as confident about the future prospects of our Medicare system. This statement is not a criticism of the care delivered by the program – just ask any senior. They love their Medicare. The problem is that, financially, it is unsustainable. As the Medicare Board of Trustees noted in their 2011 annual report, the hospital insurance fund "is not adequately financed over the next 10 years." The costs to the government are too high and the premiums paid by seniors are too low. Politically, it will be impossible for any one party to fix it. Paul Ryan, a Republican congressman from Wisconsin, introduced a plan that would save the Medicare system but would change it significantly. He was, of course, immediately excoriated by the other side.

The truth is that the Medicare shortfall is an American problem that will require an American solution. Both parties must work together to solve this and come out together with the American solution. Make no mistake: benefits will need to be reduced or limited, and premiums and taxes will most likely rise. It is simply unavoidable considering the spike in healthcare costs, especially during an individual's final six months. The answer to the Medicare dilemma will not come easily, but eventually it will be restructured for the better.

Participants in 2011: 47 million
Spending in 2011: $569 billion
Projected participants in 2021: 65 million
Projected spending in 2021: $980 billion
(Source: Congressional Budget Office)

The Rest of the World

It is a small comfort to know that we are not alone in facing large deficits and retirement anxieties. Japan's debt is larger than ours as a percentage of its GDP – and that was before the earthquake and tsunami. You have probably heard about the political unrest in Greece and Ireland over budget austerity measures that became a necessity due to huge deficits. A driving force behind these budget shortfalls involves liabilities in government-funded retirement benefits.

The European Union is facing many of the same challenges in its retirement system that we are: baby-boomer retirement, longer life spans, and reduced birthrates. According to The *Financial Times*, there are currently four workers per retiree. However, the ratio is expected to dwindle to two workers per retiree over the next 50 years. Fewer workers means less money will be available to pay for retirement benefits. The situation in Europe is exacerbated by the fact that workers there tend to retire earlier. In France, for example, the retirement age was 60. A proposal to raise it to 62 sent people into the streets! In Greece, it has not been uncommon for people in their late 40s and early 50s to retire with full pensions. Yet scaling back benefits and raising the retirement age are the only real options. Reduced benefits, though, will mean a lower standard of living unless workers come up with new approaches for closing the "pension gap."

Europe may sound depressing, but what about China? The Chinese have experienced phenomenal economic growth over the past decade and they have enjoyed huge trade surpluses with the U.S. It seems like most consumer goods are made there these days! China also purchases U.S. bonds, which enables us to fund our big deficits. However, they too are in a race with the retirement tsunami. According to the Center for Strategic and International Studies, there were 16 retirees for every 100 workers in 2005, making China a relatively young country. This ratio is expected to double to 32 retirees by 2025, and double again to 61 retirees per 100 workers by 2050! That translates into 438 million Chinese over 60 years old by mid-century. By 2030 China will actually be an older country than the U.S. with respect to the ratio of workers to retirees. It has been said that while India will get rich before it gets old, China will get old before it gets rich. This age wave could create problems for their economy and will put pressure on the government to devise solutions.

The point is, we are not the only ones going through a rough patch, and other countries may have to deal with much worse. Now is not the time to mope over what happened – instead, it is a time to look forward, look up, and find new answers to new problems.

Who Will Sign Your Retirement Paycheck?

This is not a book about how Social Security will not give you a check when you retire, or a book explaining why your company's CEO mismanaged your pension fund. It is not about the people who used to sign the checks for retirement income. This is a book about who is going to sign that retirement income check in the future.

So if neither the government nor your former employer will be signing your retirement paycheck, who will? It just might be your insurance company. Annuities (financial contracts with an insurance agency) can afford you a guaranteed income for life. In a world without stable pensions or Social Security benefits, annuities are quickly becoming a hot new item for retirement income. The June 20, 2011 cover of *Barron's* magazine focused on annuities: "With investors clamoring for steady flows of income, it's time to give annuities a fresh look." In June 2011, the Government Accountability Office released its report on Retirement Income. The full report is available online. It says that "Social Security is not enough" for people to retire on. They recommended that people "work longer, save more, and delay receipt of Social Security benefits until at least the full retirement age." It went on to say that "seniors should use a portion of their savings to purchase a lifetime income annuity to cover necessary expenses."

Now that I just spent a chapter going over every hardship, difficulty, and obstacle standing in between you and retirement, it is time to go over some solutions. Like I said earlier, I do not care for opinions. I like facts. One fact you are going to like is that you can still have the retirement of your dreams. You can have a guaranteed stream of income for the rest of your life. You can have something to give your grandkids. It is a mathematic, scientific, and economic fact that you can cover expenses and still see your savings grow.

I firmly believe in the saying that life does not close a door without opening a window. You should not worry about a lost pension or a reduced Social Security check – you should be thinking about how to expand your annuity IQ and develop an appropriate asset allocation system. There are plenty of ways to make your retirement happy and prosperous.

It is a brave new world out there, and I am here to help you find your retirement solution.

What Happened to Happily Ever After?

 Key Points from Chapter 1

1. Traditional safety nets of retirement income are changing. Pensions and Social Security will not provide the level of income your parents received. Medicare is in deep trouble.

2. The economic collapse of 2008 has shaken people's confidence. The volatility of the markets, the printing of trillions of dollars, and civil unrest around the world due to government austerity measures have all caused people to doubt the viability of their retirement.

3. These issues are affecting retirees around the world, not just in the U.S.

4. Who is going to sign YOUR monthly retirement check?

5. This book will help answer that question.

Chapter 2

The Distribution Dilemma: Just the Facts

Saving for retirement, especially in the current economic climate, can be challenging enough. However, how you draw down and distribute your retirement savings once the bell sounds and your career is over will determine whether or not you run out of money. This distribution dilemma and the various risks to your nest egg once you retire are the focus of this chapter.

Saving for Retirement: The Easy Part?

We are constantly bombarded with ads for various retirement savings plans from brokers, mutual fund companies, and financial planning firms, just to name a few. Most of these planning options focus on the accumulation phase: the time while you are working and saving for retirement. They provide you with a plethora of investment options as well as hypothetical growth rates on your principal. They will make an estimate of how much you will need to accumulate by the time you retire. You deposit a little each month into your IRA or 401(k) and gradually build up your savings to your supposed magic number.

Accumulating money is an important first step on the road to retirement. My advice is to start early and do not make assumptions that are too rosy. The sooner you can start putting money in a retirement savings account like an IRA, Roth, or 401(k), the better. No less than 15% of your income should be directed to long-term savings. As you approach retirement, try to make it 25%. "Wait till next year" might be a great sports cliché, but it is not a good plan for retirement savings. The longer you wait, the more you will have to play catch up, which means you will have to dedicate larger amounts each year to your retirement accounts. In addition, you should guard against rosy scenarios. Recent data from the U.S. Census Bureau indicates that salaries tend to plateau by your early 40s. From that point on, it is likely that you will not receive much beyond a cost-of-living adjustment. Also, if you lose a job in your 50s, it can be difficult to find another one at an equivalent salary. Given these facts, you need to save for retirement early, since you cannot count on big salary increases later in your career.

As you approach retirement, you may notice that you fixate more and more on wealth accumulation. However, accumulation is actually only a small part of the equation at this stage. Assuming you have a steady job or some other stream of income during your pre-retirement years, adding money to savings should technically be the easiest part of retirement planning. You can make up for losses in your investments by contributing more to your retirement savings, which you are not spending at the moment anyway. However, the day you retire, the rules change! Now you are spending assets instead of accumulating them. Even if you save up to your goal of $1 million or $5 million or whatever amount you decide, you could still squander it all away in poor investments or by withdrawing it too quickly. In truth, there is no magic number. The accumulation phase is only the end of the beginning, whereas the distributions from your savings must last until the end.

Distributing assets in a way that ensures you get the most out of your retirement without running out of money is a difficult balancing act, and should be taken even more seriously than accumulation. Some retirees never do anything for enjoyment in retirement. Why not? They are so afraid of losing money that they invest in ultra low-yielding investments – like passbook savings accounts or low-interest Certificates of Deposit (or, as I say, Certificates of Depreciation, given today's low interest rates) that are covered by FDIC insurance. Others may invest more wisely but will not spend a nickel for the same fear of running out of funds. Still others spend wildly in the early years of their retirement only to find out their spending, and the never-ending curse of inflation, has now relegated them to near-poverty for the rest of their years. So when planning your golden years, think less about how much you have and more about how you will spread out what you have so that it will last the rest of your life. The next section will examine the risks you need to consider when figuring out the right accumulation and distribution strategies for your retirement.

Retirement Risks

LONGEVITY RISK

People are living longer than ever before. The average 65-year-old male will live to age 85, while the average 65-year-old female will live to 88. But what's the problem with averages? The problem is that they have nothing to do with how long any one individual will live. Half of everyone reading this book will live longer than their gender's average life expectancy. Life expectancy is not an average at all; it is simply a mid-point. Half of all 65-year-old men will die prior to age 85, but the whole other half will remain alive. Half of all 65-year-old females will die prior to age 88. The other half? All alive. So averages are not at all an indicator of how long your retirement days will last – you need to operate under the notion that you very well may live long past your gender's average age of death.

Additionally, married people live longer than single people. I have no idea why, but it's a fact. If you have a husband and wife who are 65, there is a 50/50 chance that one of them will live to age 92. Think about that – think about all the 65-year-old couples you know. 50% of them will have at least one member live to 92. There is a 25% chance one of them will live to 97. So if you are married, you really need to consider joint life expectancy. And there will be plenty of people reading this book who will live beyond age 100, especially considering medical innovations and rising life expectancy rates. As reported recently in the *Wall Street Journal*, the number of Americans who live to age 100 or greater increased 43% between 2000 and 2010, to 71,991 from 50,454.

When planning for retirement income, you cannot plan to have income until age 90 – you really need to plan to have income until age 100 and possibly beyond. That may seem like playing it a bit too safe, but it is not at all unreasonable if half of retirees are already living into their 90s. Your retirement savings will probably need to last for 25 years or more. In addition, the longer you live, the more inflation can eat away at your savings if you are not careful. You will need an investment and withdrawal strategy that will last as long as you do.

Probability of a 65-Year-Old Living to:

Probability	Male	Female	One Spouse
50%	85	88	92
25%	92	94	97

Source: Annuity 2000 Mortality Table, appeared in Scott DeMonte and Lawrence Petrone, "Income Annuities Improve Portfolio Outcomes in Retirement," Financial Research Corporation report, 2010.

LONGEVITY IS A "RISK MULTIPLIER"

It is also important to understand that longevity is not just a risk. It is a multiplier of the other risks. Because of this, it is imperative that you transfer that risk to an insurance company. Because insurance companies utilize risk pooling, they are perfectly positioned to manage longevity risk. The risk when companies sell life insurance is that someone dies too soon; the risk when they sell a lifetime income annuity is that someone lives too long. Because they are on both sides of the risk, they perfectly hedge longevity risk. No other industry can do this. Let me explain why removing longevity risk is so important to the success of your retirement.

If you retire at age 65 and die at age 68, it would not

matter if the stock market dropped 40%. It would not have mattered if you had withdrawn 12% per year, or if inflation increased by double digits, or if you did not buy a long-term care policy. You did not live long enough for any of that to matter. However, if you live to age 100, any one of those things would have devastated your retirement. The risks of needing long-term care skyrocket with longevity. So if you ask me what the biggest risk in retirement is, I would say that hands down it is longevity risk, simply because it has a multiplier effect on all of the other risks.

WITHDRAWAL RATE RISK

Another fact I have observed: people know how much money they have. Given the volatility in the financial markets in recent years, I have updated that observation a bit: now I say people know how much money they *had*. But in all seriousness, I do believe people still know how much money they have. With online banking and other financial services that have sprung up over the past few decades, it has become increasingly easy for upcoming retirees to keep full track of their finances. The real problem is that once people have a good idea of how much they have saved, they are not quite sure what to expect from it or how to use it. Distribution strategies play a key role here, so it is paramount that you take into account withdrawal rate risk.

The amount you distribute or withdraw from your retirement savings, when examined in conjunction with your lifespan, will determine whether you live comfortably or run out of money. Let us look at a simple example without factoring in inflation or investment performance. Suppose you retired at 65 with $100,000 in retirement savings and started withdrawing about $5,000 per year (5%). If you lived for 10 more years, you would still have $50,000 left to pass on to your loved ones. However, if you lived 30 more years to age 95, and withdrew that same amount ($5,000 per year), you would be out of money by age 85! The next 10 years would be tough since your retirement savings would be exhausted. The bottom line is that the longer you live, the greater the risk to depleting your savings unless you adjust your withdrawal rates downward.

MetLife did a study about this in 2008. It said that 43% of all baby boomers believe they can take out 10% per year or more from their portfolio in retirement. Well, you can, but you're going to run out of money very quickly. *The Wall Street Journal* had another article that explained the bulletproof withdrawal rate for a diversified portfolio. What is your guess, 5%? Wrong – too much. Even a 4% withdrawal rate fails 20 to 30% of the time depending on what investment model and assumptions you use. So what is the bulletproof rate? Only 2%! *The Wall Street Journal* said that 2% is the bulletproof withdrawal rate, although 3% is considered safe. Alternatively, 4% is pushing it, and with 5% or more you will probably run out of money – it is only a matter of time. Most people have no idea how dangerous it is to withdraw too much each year. You see, after longevity risk, withdrawal rate risk is one of the biggest challenges you will face in retirement.

ORDER OF RETURN RISK

As you surely know, the market can take swift turns up and down. What matters to you, however, is the average return from your investments over a period of years. But the day you retire and start taking money out of a portfolio, all the rules change and average returns are no longer important. This statement probably goes against what most retirees think. It certainly goes against what you have experienced, because for your whole life, you have been a saver and an investor. You have grown used to checking the average returns on your IRA, your 401(k), your stocks, and your bonds. If you can get a 3% average return, it's better than 1%. And if you can get 5%, it's of course better than 3%. So we grow up thinking that average returns are what really matter.

You might be thinking like Jim. The year was 1973. He had $100,000. He invested 50% in stocks and 50% in bonds. Over the following 22 years, Jim averaged a 10.1% return per year! His money grew to approximately $846,000 – and it does not matter if we run the numbers backwards from 1995 to 1973 because he still averaged 10.1% per year. Jim still wound up with a boatload of money regardless of the sequence of his yearly returns.

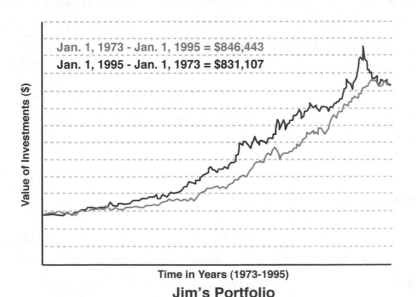

Jim's Portfolio

Source: New York Life Investment Management LLC, 2004

That's the way that some people think the world works, but it does not work that way the day you retire. Consider Bill, who also had $100,000 in 1973. Just like Jim, he invested 50% of it in stocks and the other half in bonds. He also averaged 10.1% a year for 22 years. However, Bill retired in 1973 and needed income, so his financial advisor told him he could take out 5% per year. With an average yearly return of twice that, both Bill and his advisor figured everything would be fine. The result? He is dead broke. Now you are wondering, how can you average 10.1% a year for 22 years, take out 5% a year, and go broke? The short answer is that average returns don't matter – the 10.1% yearly average has nothing to do with the sequence, or order, of returns over the years. The day you retire, there is only one thing that matters, and that is the order of those returns.

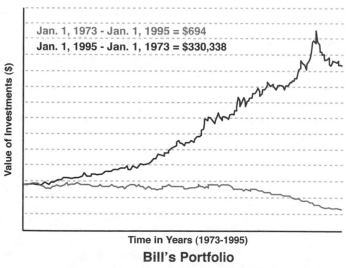

Jan. 1, 1973 - Jan. 1, 1995 = $694
Jan. 1, 1995 - Jan. 1, 1973 = $330,338

Value of Investments ($)

Time in Years (1973-1995)
Bill's Portfolio

Source: New York Life Investment Management LLC, 2004

You may remember what happened to the stock market between 1973 and 1975: the market went down for three consecutive years. Here's the deal: if the market goes down for the first few years of your retirement (assuming your assets are in a diversified portfolio), you are going to be in trouble. You will either have to put in more, take out less, or you will run out of money. The order of returns is crucial in this scenario; losses in the first few years of retirement can devastate your portfolio.

Take a look at the chart below; this is also going to oppose everything you have been taught. I think almost all financial advisors were taught that the older you are, the more conservatively you should invest. For example, that an 80-year-old should invest more conservatively than a 60-year-old and that the 60-year-old should invest more conservatively than a 40-year-old. However, that is *not* what this chart shows. Both of these portfolios have identical "average returns." What is the difference between the two portfolios? The dark line shows the portfolio that lost money early in retirement, and you can see that it devastated these people's retirement. The lighter line shows a portfolio that lost money later in retirement, and it had much less of an impact on the person's retirement.

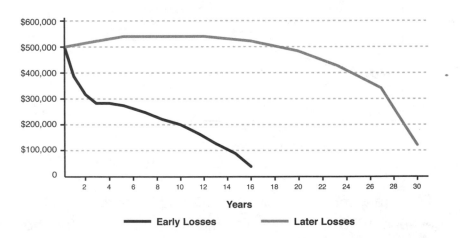

Source: New York Life Investment Management LLC, 2004

This chart shows the results of:

	Year 1	Year 2	Year 3
Early losses	-15%	-10%	-5%
	Year 28	Year 29	Year 30
Later losses	-15%	-10%	-5%

- The hypothetical example assumes a $500,000 initial balance and $25,000 annual withdrawals.

- Withdrawals are adjusted each year by 3% for inflation.

- This hypothetical example assumes an annual 6.3% rate of return in each year that the account does not have losses, and it does not take into account taxes.

- This example is hypothetical and does not represent the performance of an actual investment.

A recent study by the Government Accountability Office (June 2011) discussed the order of returns risk and provided the following example based on a $100,000 initial investment at age 65 and assumes a 9% annual withdrawal rate. It also projected that the returns below would repeat every three years. The chart on the next page shows how long an investment with a 7% average annual return could last depending on the order of the returns. The report noted that "if the sequence of returns in the second and third year were reversed, holding all else constant, the average annual return would be the same; yet if withdrawals are made each year, savings would be depleted sooner with the first sequence of returns." This example illustrates the danger of depending on a volatile stock market when you need retirement income. Even an up market may not provide the security you need once you retire and start taking out money.

Year 1	Year 2	Year 3	Ave. Return	Years Until Depleted
+7%	-13%	+27%	+7%	18
+7%	+27%	-13%	+7%	24

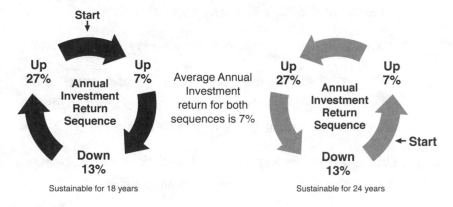

Source: GAO Report - Retirement Income, June 2011, p. 16

The order of returns risk is greatest in the years right before and right after you retire. Big market declines, like we saw in 2008-2009, that occur during this timeframe could be devastating to your retirement savings and future income. Many advisors believe the older you are, the more conservative your investments should be. But in reality, the years right before and after the beginning of your retirement matter far more than those later years. So if you asked me, "Tom, when is the riskiest, most critical time for a retiree, when they really should not mess anything up?" It is right here. If you want to pick a time in your life to not lose money, that period would be the last five or six years that you are working and the first five or six years of retirement.

Prudential made this concept famous with their "Retirement Red Zone®," and they were absolutely right.

Market risk is greatest in years just before and after retirement

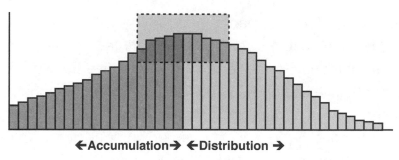

←Accumulation→ ←Distribution →

Source: New York Life Investment Management LLC, 2004

INFLATION RISK

One risk that will almost certainly affect every retirement portfolio is inflation, which can decimate purchasing power over time. For example, if you get $3,000 per month from your nest egg, the purchasing power at 4% inflation will be cut by more than half in 20 years and by more than two-thirds in 30 years. Even if inflation averages only 3% per year over the next 15 years, you will need about $4,700 per month to match the purchasing power of $3,000 in today's dollars. However, there have been some periods, such as the late 1970s, when inflation soared into the double digits.

Inflation is extremely problematic for retirees who are on fixed incomes and who are depending on their retirement savings to help make ends meet. High inflation can erode both your income and your portfolio if you do not plan for it. The U.S. has experienced a period of relative price stability and low inflation for the past 25 years or so. Even so, prices of food, gas, postage, and other items you buy have gone up significantly over this same period. Many Americans are very worried about inflation right now, especially considering the recent activities of the Federal Reserve in the aftermath of the financial panic.

Over the past few years, the Fed printed nearly $3 trillion worth of money in the form of "Quantitative Easing 1" and "Quantitative Easing 2." I know not all of you are economics majors, but what happens to the value of a dollar every time you print another dollar? It goes down. Well, if the value of the dollar goes down, what happens when you go to buy something? You need more dollars. This is inflation. When the government prints money, it causes inflation – eventually. But what many people do not realize is that printing money alone does not cause inflation. Mr. Bernanke, the Federal Reserve chairman, could print $5 trillion, but if he dug a hole and buried it, there would be no inflation. The money has to make its way into the economy to have any impact on inflation.

This second and equally important component of inflation is called the velocity of money. It is a measurement of how fast money turns over in the economy based on the amount of economic activity. If we assumed normal money velocity, the Fed's printing of nearly $3 trillion would have not only caused inflation, but hyperinflation. But these are not normal times, and economic activity has plunged due to the recession and ensuing rise in unemployment. Therefore, the money that the government has printed has not fully worked its way into the economy.

Some economists will say that the Fed's policy has worked its way into commodity markets, causing oil, gas, gold, silver, and agricultural product prices to soar. We will find out soon how all of that ends. The website SeekingAlpha.com recently had an article I found to be quite timely. It read, "What we are seeing right now is inflation in everything you OWE (like food, gas, and medicine) and deflation in everything you OWN (like real estate)." They went on to call it a "toxic combination."

It is extremely important for you to protect your retirement assets from inflation, since inflation increases the risk that you will run out of money. There are financial strategies to deal with inflation during retirement such as purchasing inflation protection on a lifetime income annuity. In addition, you can self-insure your portfolio against inflation by boosting your retirement savings while you are still working. Suppose your goal was to save $100,000 for retirement. You could get 25 years of inflation protection for your annual withdrawals if you started your retirement with $160,000, assuming a 3% inflation rate and 6% average return on your portfolio.

DEFLATION RISK

Deflation might be just as big a risk to retirees as inflation. Deflation is the reverse of inflation and means a decline in the overall price of goods and services. You may be wondering, why would declining prices be a bad thing? There are several reasons. First, deflation or falling prices would cause a dramatic slowdown in economic activity. Consumers and businesses would be reluctant to spend or borrow. Think about it: why buy something today if you could purchase the same item six months later for a lot less? You could just hoard your cash. Second, deflation would lead to a decline in wages and eventually trigger large job losses. In order to get workers to accept falling wages, companies would be forced to lay off large numbers of people. These factors in turn would drive us into a deep recession. Could we be in for a dangerous bout of deflation?

Deflation is triggered by a decline in the overall level of demand in the economy. Less demand translates to lower prices. As you have no doubt observed, falling prices are not a bad thing if they are due to mass production and/or cheaper overseas labor. Just visit a local Walmart. However, if price declines are caused by a lack of demand, the economy stagnates and contracts. We have already seen this happen in the real estate sector, and prices have tanked accordingly. However, there is another bubble ready to burst: I call it the government bubble. Governments around the world for the past 30 years have over-promised, and for the next 30 years they will be in the business of under-delivering. The deflationary impact of these changes in government policy could be devastating.

Recall that many foreign governments such as France, Ireland, and Greece have been cutting pensions and making changes to retirement plans. An analyst on the website SeekingAlpha.com actually recommended investing in tear gas. Can you believe that? As governments around the globe are forced to cut their programs, the number of riots and protests requiring police intervention and tear gas will spike. Beyond the political chaos, all of these government cuts will deflate the economy since there will be less money to spend.

Now, is this government bubble just overseas? No. Look at California, New York, New Jersey, Illinois – many of these states are nearly bankrupt. On the state and local level, we are facing about $3 trillion of unfunded government pensions. So there are going to have to be cuts upon cuts at the local level as well as cuts upon cuts at the state level. The town I live in, for instance, recently laid off 50 government employees. My town is obviously not the only one. In fact, you will see somewhere between 1 million and 2 million government employees at the local, state, and federal levels laid off in the next 10 years. These layoffs will mean less money being spent in the overall economy, a reality that can cause deflation.

Speaking of the federal level, by the time you read this our country will be nearly $15 trillion in debt. With Social Security and Medicare, there are another $40 trillion of unfunded benefits to reckon with. Add Medicaid and now we are close to $68 trillion. Needless to say, an extraordinary number of cuts will be made. These cuts in government spending are deflationary – less money in the economy means reduced demand and falling prices.

One Trillion Dollars – By the Numbers

Most people don't really know what a trillion is. After all, it rhymes with million and billion. Here is a very simple way to understand how much a trillion is: if one dollar equals one second, a million dollars would be about 11.5 days, and a billion dollars would be 32 years. A trillion dollars would be 32,000 years. Isn't that incredible – 32,000 years...

There are also problems in the private sector that could cause deflation. I already mentioned the real estate crash. In addition, there are two other trends that point to decreased consumer demand and lower overall prices. Consider all of the mortgage debt, credit card debt, student loan debt, and corporate debt. All of this debt must be deleveraged (paid down or reduced) to the tune of $25 to $45 trillion! This deleveraging is highly deflationary. All of the foreclosures and short sales in the real estate sector are like putting money through a shredder. While everyone is watching the Federal Reserve printing money on the front side, they do not see all of the shredding of money on the backside. Home prices continue to decline, housing starts are at record lows, home vacancies near record highs – all of this is very deflationary. The unemployment and underemployment numbers are some of the worst we have seen in the post-World War II era.

On top of all this, baby boomers are now officially over the hill when it comes to spending money. You will typically spend the most money between the ages of 45 and 50. This period is when you have two kids in college, two brand new cars, and the biggest home you have ever had. For years, baby boomers drove this economy as they wanted more, and bigger, and better, everything. Now, however, boomers are well past their peak spending years, meaning they will spend less and less as they age. As we have noted, less spending means reduced demand, which is deflationary.

I never said, of course, that I could predict the future. But the bond market does, or at least tries, to do this every single day. You really have to watch the bond market. If you see interest rates rising, the smart money is seeing the possibility of future inflation. If you see interest rates falling, then expect possible deflation. What you are really looking for is one word: growth. If you see the economy picking up, unemployment falling, the housing market recovering, or the stock market rising, then the risk is inflation since money velocity will pick up. Remember, homes are "real assets," which is why they are called "real estate." Real assets typically go up in times of inflation, not down. If you are looking for an inflection point where inflation and higher interest rates could happen, look for when unemployment numbers drop and housing prices bottom and start to move higher.

On the other hand, if you see a double-dip in housing, the stock market crashing, and unemployment rising, the risk is deflation. It has become my mantra: these are not normal times. You have to be aware like never before. You cannot just "go with the flow." All of these economic headwinds are exactly why you need this book right now. So now that I have you good and depressed, are there any solutions? Yes, the rest of this book will focus on solutions.

The Distribution Dilemma: Just the Facts

 Key Points from Chapter 2

1. Accumulating money may be the easiest part of retirement. Start early and save as much as you can – 15% of your income would be a good start.

2. Understand that longevity is not just a risk in retirement, it is a RISK MULTIPLIER of the other risks.

3. The withdrawal rate risk is the risk of running out of money by taking too much out of your retirement savings each year. A 2% withdrawal rate is considered bulletproof, 3% is safe. Withdrawing 4% or more a year can cause your portfolio to run out of money.

4. Understand how the order of returns can have a dramatic impact on portfolio success.

5. The riskiest time to invest is right before or right after retirement. A loss during these years can have a devastating impact on your retirement savings.

6. Inflation is a risk that increases over time. With the amount of money the Federal Reserve has printed and injected into the economy, if we get any money velocity (increase in economic activity), we could see significant inflation.

7. Deflation may be the biggest risk in the short term. Governments around the world are cutting budgets and benefits. U.S. consumers are reducing their debts. Housing is still a mess. Unemployment and underemployment are too high – all of this is deflationary.

Chapter 3

Guaranteed Paychecks and Playchecks

Income You Can Count On

The life insurance industry was built for markets like the ones we are facing now – life insurance and annuities can be the solution to many of today's personal finance dilemmas, as these products are based on math and science. There are a wide variety of annuities out there, and we will examine all of them in a later chapter. Right now, we are going to look closely at one: the lifetime income annuity. Many companies call it a SPIA – a Single Premium Immediate Annuity. It is an annuity that provides immediate, guaranteed income for life. I cannot stress enough how important this product is to a successful retirement. In fact, in order to retire in an optimal manner, you have to use this type of annuity.

For a moment, pretend I am your retirement planner so I can show you how simple this is. I am recommending that you purchase a lifetime income annuity so that you can have a great retirement. And the first thing you will probably ask me is, "Well, Tom, what is a lifetime income annuity?" Here are the words I use: it's a guaranteed paycheck for life. That's all it is: a guaranteed paycheck for life.

To make this even easier to understand, let me remind you that you already have a lifetime income annuity – your Social Security check. Remember, Social Security is simply a guaranteed paycheck for life. If you have a pension, that is also a guaranteed paycheck for life. Social Security and pensions are examples of lifetime income annuities.

The Importance of the Playcheck

Now every once in a while, I come across someone who says, "I don't need another guaranteed paycheck. I worked for Boeing for 37 years. I already have a pension – I've got that covered." Then I just smile and say, "OK, you have the paycheck. But do you know what you need now? You need a guaranteed playcheck." See, I think seniors today need both a guaranteed paycheck and, perhaps just as importantly, a guaranteed "playcheck." Let me prove it to you.

On what day of the week do you spend the most money right now? What day of the week do you go golfing, go to Home Depot, go to the spa, go shopping? For most of us, that day would be Saturday – and remember, when you retire, every single day is Saturday. Many boomers are not going to need less money once they retire; they are in fact going to need more money. So I would say that you do not need just a guaranteed paycheck, but a guaranteed playcheck as well. That's all a lifetime income annuity is.

Social Security & Pension – Weak Legs of the Stool

Historically, the ideal retirement consisted of three basically equal components – Social Security, a company pension, and personal savings. This was typically illustrated graphically with the picture of a three-legged stool such as the one below. Today, however, there are problems with all three legs. Social Security, as we have discussed, is on shaky financial ground. While I have no doubt that you will receive Social Security benefits in retirement, you will not get what your parents received, and you definitely will not see as much inflation protection as your parents saw. The company pension plan, as we discussed earlier, is becoming extinct to almost everyone other than government workers. Even government

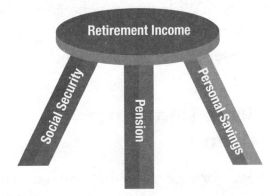

Traditional Sources of Retirement Income

What would happen if one leg was shorter than the other two?
The stool, which represents your retirement income, would lack stability.

Source: New York Life Insurance Company

workers will see significant reductions in the payouts they thought they would receive. So that only leaves the third and final leg – personal savings.

Faced with the daunting possibility of having to rely more and more on personal savings, you will probably consider the usual investment options. A Certificate of Deposit may sound like a solid move, for example, since it is FDIC insured and you can sign up at your local bank. However, I am going to go ahead and put a nail in the CD coffin for anything other than short-term needs. There is almost no reason for you to invest your hard-earned money in a CD.

Let's take a closer look at CDs – their interest rates as of late have been nothing short of pathetic. The average return on a one-year CD is presently a measly 0.36%. A two-year CD? About 0.67%. Do not spend it all in one place! Money market funds are not faring too much better. You know what mine is paying? Only 0.01%. That gives me 29 cents a month on a $35,000 balance in my money market account – absolutely ridiculous.

Other alternatives might include stocks, bonds, mutual funds, or ETFs. However, these products bring market risk back into the equation. While that may be fine while you are building your savings, it will not give you much peace of mind if you are taking money out for income during a market crash.

Why Annuities Win Out: Mortality Credits

At this point, I hope, for your sake, that you have limited any major CD or money market investments your advisors may have offered to short-term needs only. Your CPA may now be recommending tax-free municipal bonds, and your stockbroker may be suggesting high dividend paying stocks. Why settle for a boring old lifetime income annuity when you could buy bonds or stocks instead? To know why, check out the annuity payout rates of almost every insurance company in America. Did you know that at age 65, you are guaranteed about 7% a year for the rest of your life? At 75, you are guaranteed about 9% a year for the rest of your life. And once you reach 85, you are guaranteed almost 13% every year for the rest of your life. (Note that these payout rates will change when interest rates change or products are re-priced.)

Issue Age	Annual Payout Rate
65	6.7%
75	8.9%
85	12.7%

Source: New York Life Insurance Company. Sample rates, actual rates may vary.

For those of you still more inclined to invest in bank products: do banks offer different interest rates based on age? No, they pay everyone the same rate. As do bonds. Your CPA may say that she likes tax-free bonds, but they also pay everyone the same rate. Finally, ask your stockbroker: do stocks pay higher dividends based on your age? No!

So here is an important concept to understand: a lifetime income annuity has higher payout rates based on age because the annuity holder gets paid mortality credits. In effect, the main reason you want to buy a lifetime income annuity is because you get paid mortality credits. CDs pay no mortality credits. Tax-free bonds do not pay mortality credits. Stocks have never paid a mortality credit in the history of the stock market. Lifetime income annuities are structured to satisfy the needs of aging clients, and that is why annuities are the only financial product that offers mortality credits. Dr. Moshe Milevsky refers to these mortality credits as "longevity credits" because you actually get paid for living longer! (See Appendix.)

What are mortality credits, exactly? Basically, they are a financial reward that increases the longer you live. The more years you spend holding a lifetime income annuity, the more mortality credits you will be paid. These have nothing to do with stocks or interest rate returns. Instead, it is an actuarial calculation by the insurance company, based on your age and gender, that adds a credit from the entire risk pool of everyone who buys the same type of lifetime income annuity. This may sound a little confusing, but it really is not. Life insurance companies know when people are going to die. Now they do not know when *you* are going to die, but they know almost exactly how long 100 people just like you will live as a group. Because of that, the insurance companies can pay each person as though they knew when each person is going to die. Because some people will die early and will not collect income for that long, they can pay the entire pool a little more than a traditional investment.

I know what some of you are thinking: "What if I'm one of the first ones to go? I don't want my money to disappear when I die." But consider this: does your money have to disappear when you die? Not at all – you can do joint life. Joint life with your spouse, joint life with your kids, joint life with your grandkids. You can choose life with 20 years certain payments, life with 30 years certain payments, life with guaranteed death benefit, or life with cash refund. Less than 10% of lifetime income annuities sold are life-only – the money disappears when you die. Almost everyone wants a guarantee that their money will outlast them somehow. These guarantees are available with annuities, but they will reduce your income payments. The older you are, the longer you live, and the fewer guarantees you choose, the more mortality credits you will be paid and the higher your annual income payment will be.

 ## Goal: Providing Income Across Generations

I recently did a seminar at the IMAX theater in San Antonio, Texas for an audience of about 400 people. When I finished, an 83-year-old gentleman approached me. He said, "Well, Tom, that was a very interesting presentation. But what should I do with my money?" And so I asked him two fundamental questions: what do you want your money to do while you're alive, and what do you want it to do when you die? And here's what he said: "Well, I reckon nobody's ever asked me that before. But here's what I want: I want a guaranteed paycheck every month for the rest of my life. And when I die, I want my wife to get that same check for the rest of her life. Now when she dies, we want our son to get that same check for the rest of his life. And then when he dies, I suppose his wife should get it for the rest of her life. And finally, when his wife dies, we want our granddaughter to get it for the rest of her life. That's what I want." Lucky for him, he can accomplish all of this with just one lifetime income annuity. Here is how:

1. Joint Annuitants are Grandpa and the granddaughter.

2. Grandma is named as successor owner.

3. When Grandpa dies, Grandma names the son as the successor owner.

4. When Grandma dies, the son names his wife as the successor owner.

5. When both the husband and wife die, the checks will go to the granddaughter for the rest of her life.

6. When both Grandpa and the granddaughter die, the checks will cease.*

*This, of course, assumes that the granddaughter will live longer than her parents and grandparents.

Components of Lifetime Income Payout
Male age 65, $100,000 investment

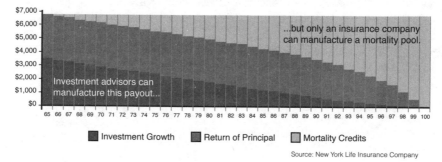

Source: New York Life Insurance Company

There are three parts to a lifetime income annuity paycheck. The first part is principal (that is the medium grey in the middle). The second part is interest, which is the lower dark portion. Investment advisors using stock or bond funds can give you both principal and interest. But what they cannot do without an insurance company is pay mortality credits. That is the extra income indicated in the lightest area at the top.

OTHER PEOPLE'S MONEY

Here is another way to think of mortality credits. A financial advisor told me that many of his clients had not saved enough money for retirement. There was no way they could use stocks, bonds, or CDs to withdraw enough money without a high probability of running out of money. He told his clients the best chance they had was to pool their money with a group of other people who also had not saved enough. If they all selected "life only" payouts, the payout rates would be high enough for them to have a decent chance at a successful retirement. As people died, some of their money, in effect, went to those who were still alive. The financial advisor called the mortality credits "other people's money." These people had decided it would be better to "leave some money on the table" if they died early rather than running out of money while alive. I believe, unfortunately, that many baby boomers will find themselves in a similar situation.

What Do You Want Your Money To Do?

Before you can begin planning a successful retirement, you must ask yourself two fundamental questions: (1) what do I need my money to do, and (2) what do I want it to do? As surprising as it may seem, many retirees cannot confidently answer either of these questions.

You need to identify what expenses you need to consider to satisfy both your needs and your desires. Then you must consider your options for covering these expenses with guaranteed sources of income.

Know What Your Basic Expenses Are

Luckily, the answer to the first question should be the same for all retirees – you need your money to cover your basic living expenses. I realize these costs are not what most people think about when contemplating retirement. But they are an essential part of a successful retirement plan. What these costs entail will vary for each individual, but will usually comprise a combination of the following:

Housing: Whether you have yet to finish paying off your mortgage or you simply pay rent every month, housing costs can be a significant expense for many retirees. When determining your monthly living cost, be sure to include the money you spend on utilities, internet, television, and upkeep on top of your rent or mortgage payment. If you have been lucky enough to completely pay off your house, you still must consider property taxes and repairs. Do not leave any basic living expenses out of your budget – they are the most important.

Health: Medical bills can often exceed even housing costs, so it is paramount that you weigh in the funds that you will need for prescription drugs, handicapped accommodation, surgeries, and perhaps long-term care. I cannot stress enough that Medicare and Medicaid alone will not be able to sufficiently cover your health costs as you grow older. Setting aside money specifically for health insurance, long-term care insurance, and unexpected events is a must for retirees.

Food and Personal Spending: Figure out how much money you spend monthly on groceries and dining out. You will also want to factor in how much you spend on hygiene products and other amenities – basically everything that you buy and need on a regular basis. Some people spend $200 a week on groceries without even realizing what a large chunk of their budget they are spending.

Transportation: If you do not own a car, transportation costs should hopefully remain quite low (occasional bus, train, or plane fare, but nothing more). Car owners, however, must be wary of the expenses they will continue to incur throughout retirement. These include the skyrocketing price of gas as well as auto loan and auto insurance payments. Additionally, the sudden need for repairs or maintenance can compound standard transportation costs.

Debt: If you have any outstanding loans – be it anything from your child's college tuition to credit card debt – it is imperative to account for this in your basic expenses budget. You can also look at ways to consolidate debt or reduce interest payments. (If it is paid off by the time you retire, you are fine.)

The Importance of Playchecks

When you think about retirement, what do you usually think of? Some people will say travel. Others will say golf or gardening. Others just want to have time to do all of the things they never had time to do. Most people would probably not say, "Being able to buy groceries or pay my mortgage or pay for health insurance." Paying for basic living expenses is an important step, but it is only the beginning.

This is where the second question comes into play: what do you *want* your money to do? Once you have retired, there is no more 9-to-5. You are no longer tied to an office five days a week. Every day is Saturday, meaning your number of opportunities to have fun has risen dramatically. How you spend this time, and how you spend your money during this time, is entirely up to you, whether it is spent golfing or traveling or lounging on your porch all day. You need to make allowance for the fun stuff in your retirement plan as well. I call income for these activities "playchecks."

Guaranteed Sources of Income

Now that you have determined your basic expenses and the amount you will spend on them each month, it is time to figure out how much income you will have. When you get right down to it, retirement planning is a fairly simple equation: make sure your income sources are greater than your expenses. First, you will want to subtract your expected Social Security benefits and (if applicable) pension payments from your monthly costs. In all likelihood, these monthly benefits will not cover all of your projected basic living expenses. Still, if you are lucky enough to receive them, you can use them toward paying down your average monthly costs.

Whatever the shortfall is, after you account for Social Security and pension benefits, will need to come from your retirement savings. What is the best way to pay off these costs each month? Certificates of Deposit and money market funds are paying less than 1% at the moment, so these surely are not efficient methods to pay for basic expenses. Stocks and bonds are subject to market volatility. They definitely seem like a good way to pay when markets are going up, but they are highly risky since withdrawals lock in losses during down markets. Those who continue to withdraw during a down market will run out of funds most quickly.

What retirees need much more than the above products are guaranteed sources of income on which they can depend every month. In addition to pensions and Social Security, it is quite possible that you will need a third source of income to cover all of your costs. Here is what you need to do: fill in any shortfalls with a lifetime income annuity from a financially strong insurance company. This strategy will guarantee you steady paychecks for the rest of your life. Remember, you also need to have playchecks to cover the fun stuff beyond the basics. Even if most of your basic expenses are covered by Social Security and pension income, a lifetime income annuity can provide you with a stable source of guaranteed paychecks and playchecks.

Even if you only invested $100,000 into a lifetime income annuity, you could still set yourself up with a dependable monthly check and an impressive payout. Add on a 10-year payment guarantee and have that $100,000 guaranteed to pay your beneficiary for up to 10 years in the case of an early death. A cash refund option guarantees that you will get paid for life and your beneficiaries will receive a cash refund of the difference between your investment and the money that you received while alive. Annuities provide flexible options that can be tailored to your investment objectives.

_100,000_

Buyer	Annuity for Life		w/10-yr Guarantee		w/Cash Refund	
	Monthly Check	Payout Rate	Monthly Check	Payout Rate	Monthly Check	Payout Rate
65-yr-old man	$557	6.7%	$555	6.6%	$525	6.3%
65-yr-old woman	$558	6.7%	$549	6.6%	$518	6.2%
70-yr-old man	$629	7.6%	$626	7.5%	$574	6.9%
70-yr-old woman	$628	7.5%	$609	7.3%	$566	6.8%
75-yr-old man	$731	8.8%	$709	8.5%	$637	7.7%
75-yr-old woman	$730	8.8%	$685	8.2%	$628	7.5%

Source: New York Life Insurance Company (as of July 16, 2011; note that these payout rates can change every two weeks so contact a financial advisor for an up-to-date-quote.)

In addition, you need to budget so that you do not spend more than what you have for any particular month. Remember, you have to plan for retirement as if you will live to 100. According to _The Wall Street Journal_, the number of Americans living to age 100 or greater increased a whopping 43% between 2000 and 2010.

Optimizing Your Portfolio

Now that you have paychecks and playchecks covering all of your basic expenses, you may be wondering what to do with the rest of your savings. The best strategy here is to optimize your portfolio – but this task is ultimately more complicated than it seems. Everyone optimizes their portfolio slightly differently. Financial services companies have programs that ask fourteen simple questions, most along the lines of, "How old are you?" and, "How much do you want to leave to your children?" They then develop a two-page customized portfolio optimization for which step one is to cover your basic expenses with guaranteed income. Once you have done that, they then advise you to place some money in U.S. stocks, some money in international stocks, some money in bonds, and some in cash, depending on your specific situation.

And what else? Some more guaranteed lifetime income? Yes! Because here is another fact: the day you retire, you cannot optimize your income without using a lifetime income annuity. A Ph.D. by the name of Menahem Yaari proved this back in the 1960s. Dr. Yaari discovered that "only a lifetime income annuity can optimize income over the indefinite period of a human life." (See Appendix.) Let me put that into English for the non-believers still out there. Let's assume that you choose to optimize income in retirement without using a lifetime income annuity. Answer me one question: I need to know the day you will die. I need to know the month, the day, and the year. Because if you do not know when you are going to die, you cannot optimize income in retirement.

Think about it: if you knew you were going to die tomorrow, you could have a heck of a party tonight. But if you knew you were going to live to 100, you would have to be very careful with your money. Of course, you cannot predict the exact time you will die. But luckily, life insurance companies can conduct actuarial calculations to determine your life expectancy. They do not know when each one of you individually will die, but they do know how long any large group of people will live – almost to the exact day. And because they know how long everyone reading this book is likely to live, they can pay each and every one of you as though they knew exactly when each of you will die. An insurance company can optimize your income in retirement. You cannot do it by yourself. It is a mathematical, scientific, and economic fact.

In addition to optimizing your portfolio for lifetime income, your portfolio also needs to be optimized with a special eye on inflation protection. Commodities, stocks, real estate, mutual funds, variable annuities, and TIPS bonds are all examples of types of investments that tend to keep up with inflation, although these involve taking some market risks with your assets.

Why such a focus on inflation? Because the lifetime income annuity protects against many of the other risks that retirees face. In a deflationary environment, for instance, a lifetime income annuity is one of the best investments you can make. Your paycheck remains the same while expenses go down each year, giving you a higher annual (real) income. A lifetime income annuity also helps protect against longevity risk, since you receive a paycheck each month no matter how long you live. And lastly, a lifetime income annuity certainly protects you from market risk and withdrawal rate risk. So the major risk that remains is inflation, and a lifetime income annuity is vulnerable to inflation risk. Now, you can purchase an inflation protection rider on a lifetime income annuity and have your paycheck grow by 3% to 5% each year. This is certainly an option. Choosing inflation protection, however, results in a lower paycheck initially – sometimes significantly lower.

Portfolio Optimization in Practice

A more effective method, in my experience, is to cover basic expenses with guaranteed lifetime income and then optimize the portfolio with a special eye on inflation protection. Even conservative investors, who may shy away from commodities, real estate, and stocks, still need to seriously reconsider their aversion to risk. When it comes to inflation, which poses a significant risk to seniors, trying to avoid risk in money market funds, bank accounts, and CDs actually increases the risk of inflation, devastating your retirement income buying power over time. Remember, the FDIC will not insure you against the ravages of inflation!

By allocating a portion of your portfolio toward these inflation sensitive investments, one can optimize their portfolio to protect against inflation, so if inflation occurs, the portfolio will likely rise. When the portfolio rises, you can take some profits and purchase some more guaranteed lifetime income. Over time, markets will go up and down, and when they go up, you have the opportunity to profit and buy more guaranteed income.

So what is the net result of our efforts here? We can act to protect our assets against the ravages of deflation, inflation, hyperinflation, and even a Great Depression. Regardless of what the market does, you now can enjoy peace of mind – knowing that you are in a position to have income to cover expenses no matter what the market is doing.

One last thought – let's say you are not yet convinced that a lifetime income annuity is the mathematical solution for your retirement income. You might prefer stocks, bonds, ETFs, or real estate. But here is the problem: stocks do not know when you are going to die. Neither do bonds, real estate CDs, or ETFs. So if you invest in any of these to cover your basic expenses, I will make you a promise. You will do one of two things: you will either take out too much money, which may result in running out of money eventually, or you will take out too little and forfeit the retirement you could have had.

I know so many seniors who refuse to touch their money. These people are living a "just in case" retirement and never fully enjoy the fruits of all of their labors. Covering your basic expenses with guaranteed lifetime income and optimizing the rest of your portfolio with inflation in mind are the keys to a happy and successful retirement.

Guaranteed Paychecks and Playchecks

 Key Points from Chapter 3

1. A lifetime income annuity is a MUST for an optimal retirement.

2. When every day is Saturday, you'll also need a guaranteed PLAYCHECK!

3. CDs were never made for income.

4. It's all about the mortality credits. Because longevity risk multiplies all of the other risks, you HAVE to have mortality credits in your portfolio.

5. Know the difference between your needs and wants in retirement.

6. Cover your basic expenses with guaranteed lifetime income.

7. Optimize your portfolio with a special eye on inflation. Even conservative investors need exposure to investments that will protect them from inflation.

Chapter 4

Customized Solutions to Everyday Retirement Problems

As the sun sets on your career and every day is about to become Saturday, you will be faced with issues such as: how to effectively take required minimum distributions (RMDs) from your traditional IRA or 401(k); when to start taking Social Security; how Social Security payments are taxed; whether to convert your traditional IRA to a Roth; how to recover from a bear market; what are good alternatives to low-yielding CDs or savings accounts; and how to come up with a creative way to leave a legacy to your grandchildren and great-grandchildren.

IRAs, RMDs, and Annuities

Let's take a look at how real people are solving real problems using lifetime income annuities. Remember, these annuities allow you to put a chunk of your savings into an insurance company. But unlike an IRA, the savings do not just sit there – the insurance company invests the money and then provides you a dependable, guaranteed paycheck each month for the rest of your life.

I believe if all 70-year-olds truly understood this concept, the vast majority would choose to put their IRA money into a lifetime income annuity. Of course, anyone of any age can invest in an income annuity – even if you are only 40. There are no taxes due for transferring funds from a 401(k) or IRA into an income annuity because the annuity remains an IRA. There is no 10% withdrawal penalty, even if you start taking the income prior to age 59. (Section 72(t) of the Internal Revenue Code allows anyone of any age to take substantially equal withdrawals from their qualified money, even if they are under age 59½ if certain requirements are met.) Any age can do it. So why am I focusing on 70-year-olds? Because at age 70½, you have to take out a required minimum distribution (RMD) from your traditional IRA, 401(k), and/or any other qualified money. Look at this chart: this is the government's method for enjoying your retirement. These are the RMDs plotted on a graph for a husband and wife both age 70 with $250,000 in an IRA earning 4% annually.

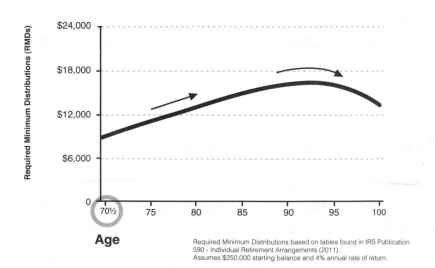

Required Minimum Distributions based on tables found in IRS Publication 590 - Individual Retirement Arrangements (2011).
Assumes $250,000 starting balance and 4% annual rate of return.

This is a withdrawal plan where the bulk of your income is taken in your nineties. This may be a great plan if your primary goal is to leave as much as possible to your heirs. But what if your goal is to take as much as you can without ever outliving your savings? If you had a blank piece of paper on which you could design your own retirement plan, is this what it would look like? I don't think so.

You are all saving money in your IRAs and 401(k)s. Why are you investing money in these accounts? You are saving it for your retirement. Hopefully, by the time you reach age 70½, you are retired. And if you're 70½, when do you think the 10 best years of your life will be? Your next 10 years will almost certainly be your best. Let's crosscheck this with the government method shown above. During the best 10 years of your retirement, according to this method, you will take out the least. I guess the government wants you to save money for your nineties so you can buy a more expensive wheelchair. And then, if you live too long past 90, your RMDs will start falling again until about age 115. Does this not strike you as odd? Would any of you design this as your own personal plan? That in the best 10 years of your life, you take out the least, and in your declining years, you take out the most? It makes no sense.

So what is the solution? A simple lifetime income annuity. If you check out the chart below, you will see the original RMDs still plotted in black. However, there is now an additional line in gray. This line displays a $250,000 joint lifetime income annuity with cash refund. That means the husband would get a check for the rest of his life, and when he dies, his wife would get the same check for the rest of her life, or vice versa. Their family is also protected in the case of premature death. For example, if they both died after receiving a total of $100,000 in payments, the family would receive a $150,000 death benefit ($250,000 initial investment – $100,000 actual payments). Many people are not even aware that they can purchase a joint life payout on qualified money. They think that IRA stands only for "Individual Retirement Account" when, in all actuality, it stands for "Individual Retirement Annuity," too. In any case, you most certainly can buy a joint life payout.

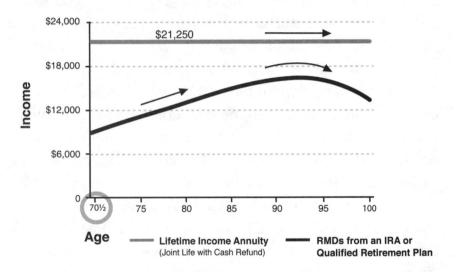

Annuity data:
New York Life Insurance Company

Required Minimum Distributions based on tables found in IRS Publication 590 - Individual Retirement Arrangements (2011). Assumes $250,000 starting balance and 4% annual rate of return.

This hypothetical example is for illustrative purposes only and based on a husband and wife, both 70 years old, with $250,000 in IRAs that earn 4% annually. Income amounts of $21,250 annually for the Lifetime Income Annuity (Joint Life with Cash Refund) are effective as of 1/12/2009. Actual amounts are dependent on interest rates in effect at time of policy issue and other parameters. Please note: A Guaranteed Lifetime Income Annuity cannot be surrendered. For qualified policies, not all payout options, features and issue ages are available due to IRS restrictions. All distributions from a qualified Guaranteed Life Income Annuity are subject to income taxes.

Continuing with this graph, you can use a Lifetime Income Annuity to add more certainty to your retirement income and satisfy the RMD's for the annuity without having to worry about calculating and withdrawing your RMDs. I have found that about 60% of 70-year-olds will choose this method immediately upon learning about it. The fact is, they need more income and had no idea they could receive income that is guaranteed to never run out. But the other 40% will say something like this: "Well, Tom, when I get that money, I've got to pay taxes, and I hate to pay taxes."

So then I have to go one step further. I say, "I understand that you don't like to pay taxes – who does? But the taxes calculated on them are just a fact of life. What you should focus on is that while you have to pay taxes, I can get you income that is stable, guaranteed, and does not fluctuate with the market or interest rates. And while doing this, you won't have to worry about calculating and withdrawing your RMDs and will have added a degree of certainty to your retirement income. Now doesn't that sound like something you should consider?"

One other concern I hear from time to time is that people want to leave their IRAs or 401(k)s to their kids. Let's backtrack – what did you invest in these for in the first place? Your retirement! You were never saving that money to give to your kids. You told me you wanted to play golf and travel the world and do all kinds of fun things as a retiree. So let me ask you a question: have you done that? Are you spending your IRA and 401(k) money to live that great retirement you wanted to? For most people, the answer is no. They did not buy a motor home, or a boat, or a country club membership. They did not even take that Alaskan cruise. When they die, what happens? The kids buy the new boat, join the country club, and take the cruise to Alaska!

Let me put it on the line here: you do not owe your kids a penny of your retirement savings. Do not even think another minute about it. Leave them the cars, the house, and whatever else is left over, but do not sacrifice your retirement for them. You raised them, and you probably helped them with college and other purchases over the years. You did more for them than they could ever repay you for. You need to spend your retirement on yourself! If you still want to give them money, then give it to them while you are alive. The guaranteed payouts from a lifetime income annuity helps you to do all of this and so much more.

When to Start Taking Social Security

When I am asked about when someone should begin accepting Social Security payments, I say that there is honestly one best answer for most people. And it is not the same answer you would probably hear from a bunch of 60- and 70-year-old men drinking their coffee at Dunkin' Donuts. If you were to ask these "wise men," you would probably hear this answer: "Sixty-two – haven't you been reading the newspapers? This country is in a huge financial mess. Get it while the getting is good – take it out at 62!"

OK, so now we know the Dunkin' Donuts answer, but is that the correct answer? Absolutely not. The correct answer is that the breadwinner of the family should delay taking Social Security payments until age 70 if possible, or at least until his or her normal retirement age (66 for some, 67 for others). The reason for this approach is simple. The breadwinner's Social Security check lasts for two lives, not one. If you take this check early, it will result in a lower paycheck for both the husband and the wife (since when the breadwinner dies, the other spouse begins receiving the breadwinner's

Social Security instead of his or her own). The recipient who made the smaller amount of money in the marriage can take it at 62, or whenever he or she wants, but the breadwinner should definitely delay.

**Monthly Benefit Amounts Differ Based on the Age
You Decide to Start Receiving Benefits**

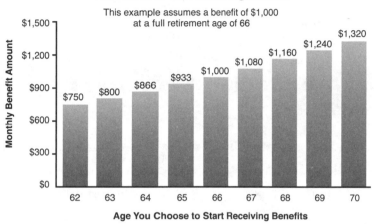

Source: Social Security Administration

One final important consideration on the matter of Social Security is health. If a retiree has a serious health condition that significantly lowers his or her odds of a long life, this person might want to take Social Security early. Once we pass away, so do our checks (except in the case of the breadwinner scenario with a surviving spouse). Thus, it makes much more financial sense to accept Social Security payments if the retiree knows he or she will not live far past 70.

I will also add that there are a number of financial advisors who have software that can demonstrate that you may be better off taking Social Security early. These monthly checks help take pressure off of withdrawals from stock and bond portfolios. In fact, this premise is much of what this entire book has been about. Remember, though, that this software creates only "hypothetical illustrations" – they can predict the future no better than anyone else. All that being said, if you are comfortable with the hypothetical rates of return and the illustration that is being provided by the advisor, I see no problem with someone taking Social Security early as part of an overall financial plan.

How Are Social Security Benefits Taxed?

Many retirees are surprised when they lose a substantial chunk of their Social Security check to taxes. Here is what you need to know: if your gross income amounts to less than $25,000 a year (excluding one-half of your Social Security benefits), none of your monthly check will be taxed. Or, if you are married and you and your spouse together make less than $32,000, you are also in the clear. However, as soon as you enter the next income brackets – which I am sure include many of you – the rules change dramatically.

Married couples that make between $32,000 and $44,000, for example, will have to pay taxes on up to 50% of their Social Security. Furthermore, couples making over $44,000 will probably pay taxes on as much as 85% of their benefits. This does not mean the federal government will take away 50% or 85% of your Social Security. The percentage only indicates the portion of your benefits that will be subject to taxation. And under federal law, the government can never tax more than 85% of your Social Security income – regardless of how much money you make.

One interesting wrinkle that can trip you up when calculating the income thresholds above is that nontaxable interest actually counts towards the total. For example, if you and your spouse have $42,000 in taxable income plus $3,000 in interest from tax-free municipal bonds, you would probably assume that only 50% of your Social Security benefit is subject to tax. However, you would be wrong! The federal government counts the tax-free interest, so your combined income would be $45,000 for purposes of calculating the Social Security benefits tax. Instead of 50%, you would have to pay tax on up to 85% of your Social Security. This policy has the effect of turning what should be tax-free income into taxable income. Annuities can help to alleviate this problem, since no taxes are paid on deferred annuities until a withdrawal is made and payments from annuities include a return of principal that is not counted as income. So many seniors are not aware that their tax-free bond interest counts toward the taxation of their Social Security benefits. When I was a financial advisor, I was able to help many seniors reduce or completely eliminate the taxation on their Social Security benefits – simply by moving tax-free bonds or CDs just sitting in the bank into deferred or income annuities. If you have a large pension or other income from an asset that cannot be moved into an annuity, you will likely be paying taxes on up to 85% of your Social Security benefits.

Once you retire and begin taking Social Security, you will receive a Social Security Benefit Statement in the mail each January for the rest of your life. If you have questions about whether you owe taxes on your Social Security, this form should be able to answer them. If it turns out that you do have to pay taxes, you have two options. Your first option is to make quarterly tax payments to the IRS each year based on your adjusted gross income. But the second option is simpler. Instead of receiving the money and then having to pay it right back to the government, you can simply opt to have the tax money withheld from your monthly Social Security checks, much like when you were working. This way, it will at least seem like that lost money never existed in the first place.

Should I Convert to a Roth IRA?

Over the years, I have had the opportunity to speak on the same platforms as John Bledsoe, an expert estate planner. He is the author of the book *The Gospel of Roth*. If you want to dig deeper on that subject, I absolutely recommend reading it. After I heard him speak, I immediately converted my IRA to a Roth IRA, and I have not once regretted that decision. In fact, John lays it out so simply that it is highly unlikely that you could ever have a regret. Why is that? Because his whole premise is that everyone should convert. No formulas, no income or tax calculations – everyone should convert! Because you can unconvert (called a recharacterization), everyone should convert with the plan of possibly "unconverting" if for some reason it turns out that the Roth does not make sense. As crazy as this initially sounds, he is right on. Since there are several dates at which you can shift the Roth IRA back to a regular one, it really may make sense to convert for some people.

There are a few key differences between a Roth and a traditional IRA. On the front end, there is the issue of tax deductibility. Contributions to a traditional IRA are tax-deductible based on income, while Roth IRA contributions are taxable.

The tax on a traditional IRA is deferred until you start taking withdrawals. However, all earnings and withdrawals in a Roth IRA are tax-free, assuming no rules or regulations have been breached. In short, you are paying tax up front with the Roth but owe no taxes later when you take the money out. Converting to a Roth basically locks you in at the current tax rates and protects you from future tax increases.

Another important difference is that traditional IRAs allow holders to withdraw beginning at age 59½ and require minimum withdrawals by age 70½. The Roth, on the other hand, possesses no mandatory distributions during the lifetime of the original owner. The Roth gives you the flexibility to decide when and how much to take out, depending on your individual tax and financial situation. In addition, since you can leave the Roth assets in place for the rest of your life, they can provide tax-sheltered growth for your family as well. Ultimately, the optimal choice is clear: you should definitely consider converting to a Roth IRA.

How to Repair Bear Market Damage

One major crisis retirees face is severe stock market downturns like those we saw in 2008 and 2009. These losses may seem nothing short of debilitating, but there is a way around them. Let's say you are a 75-year-old couple that over the past years, you have done wonderfully in the market. Your account rose from $200,000, to $400,000, to $600,000. But then, almost overnight, your account dropped back to $400,000. You got on the phone, called your broker, and uttered those famous words: get me out.

It now does not matter what anyone advises you – you refuse to leave any more funds in the market. So in your mind, the next logical step is to take the $400,000 to the bank, which kindly offers you a 1% annual return. That is only $4,000 dollars per year in income! You are depressed; you are disappointed. This money was supposed to help you and your spouse in retirement. You were going to leave some of it to your kids. It looks like the end of the road... but it is not. A rather simple strategy could save your retirement after all.

Here is what I would advise in a market loss situation such as this one. Keep about $100,000 liquid in case of emergency or financial need, and then use the other $300,000 to buy a joint lifetime income annuity that will ensure you and your spouse a paycheck for the rest of either one of your lives. The bonus? The annuity will pay you almost six times what the bank's CD will. And if one of you lives to age 100, it will even pay you all the money back that you had at the top of the market.

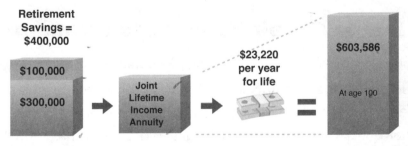

Source: New York Life Insurance Company

In addition, even if you do not think you will live to 100, you can still guarantee the return of your initial $600,000. This is what you would do: put the $400,000 into a joint lifetime income annuity with a 30 years certain payment period. If you take a look at the chart below, you may be pleasantly surprised by the guaranteed payments on the 30 years certain plan. While the annual payments are slightly lower ($21,840), over the 30-year period the payments will amount to $657,256 – even more than you had at the top of the market! And it is guaranteed for your life, your spouse's life, and goes to your kids if you and your spouse died prior to living the 30 years!

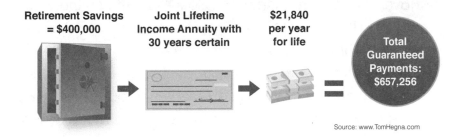

| Retirement Savings = $400,000 | Joint Lifetime Income Annuity with 30 years certain | $21,840 per year for life | Total Guaranteed Payments: $657,256 |

Source: www.TomHegna.com

Alternatives to CDs and Savings Accounts

Things look brighter now – you have solved your market crisis and left $100,000 in the bank for extra liquidity. But you still cannot help but feel that the bank's interest rates on your $100,000 investment are a little too low, even for such readily available money. If CDs and savings accounts simply do not cut it for you, there are some other options to consider.

An alternative to a bank savings product is the inflation-indexed bond. Inflation-indexed bonds are designed to protect against the inflation that causes this depreciation of assets. In the United States, they are called Treasury Inflation-Protected Securities, or TIPS, as they are issued exclusively by the U.S. Treasury. The primary benefit of TIPS? Their principal adjusts according to the Consumer Price Index, the nation's standard measure of inflation. This works out nicely for times of great inflation, because the principal in an inflation-protected security rises as the CPI rises. Some people do not believe that the CPI is a true measure of inflation since it does not count food or energy and the method of calculating the CPI has been changed by the government more than once. So keep that in mind when comparing TIPS against other inflation hedges like gold, silver, other commodities, and real estate.

Another alternative, especially for those who feel they have too much rotting in liquid reserves, would be to buy a fixed-period immediate income annuity. These are not for life; they instead generate guaranteed income over a shorter, fixed period of time, such as five or ten years. Investing a chunk of your reserves into one of these could set you up with quite the playcheck, and absolutely a better payout rate than whatever the bank offers on CDs when you consider the interest earned and return of premium. While these don't come with FDIC insurance and are not as liquid as CDs, it is a short-term commitment for a smaller portion of money – a smart way to increase your payout without totally eliminating liquidity and future investment possibilities. Remember, though, that the entire amount that went into the fixed period annuity gets paid out with no principal remaining.

Many among you may feel uneasy about ceding the liquidity of your money to whichever institution manages your IRA or annuity. Having complete control over one's money, however, does not generate nearly as much income in the end. In general, the retirees who run out of money are exactly those who wanted to be in control and keep all or much of their money liquid. Remember, liquidity is not a one-time event – it is a lifetime event. By covering your basic expenses with guaranteed income, you increase your liquidity over your lifetime. By giving up control of some of your money, you gain control over many of the risks in retirement – longevity risk, deflation risk, market risk, withdrawal rate risk, and order of returns risk. These are all risks that you cannot manage when you are trying to control your principal by keeping it in liquid assets. You may very well earn more over time and maintain more liquidity of your other assets, too.

Too many people have a false sense of liquidity – they keep their money in bonds or CDs and use the interest for income. Simultaneously, they count the principal in these accounts as liquid. Yet, if they were to liquidate this money, they would lose their income because there would be no more interest to collect! This common double counting of assets is a myth that puts many seniors at risk of running out of money.

Enter the Lifetime Income Annuity

	CD	Lifetime Income Annuity
Initial Investment	$100,000	$100,000
CD Rate of return / Annuity payout rate	1.75%	6.04%
Total annual income	$1,750	$6,040
Tax-free income	$0	$3,962
Taxes owed	$490	$582
After-tax income	$1,260	$5,458

(See note on next page)

** For the lifetime of both spouses. The annual Lifetime Income Annuity payments are guaranteed, regardless of the volatility of the market. At the time of the second spouse's death, the Cash Refund option returns to beneficiaries any difference between the initial premium ($100,000) and the total amount paid out. At the end of the maturity term, the full investment amount of the CD plus interest becomes available again, whereas with a Lifetime Income Annuity, the annual payment each year includes both interest and principal. Sample rates, actual rates will vary.

(Source: New York Life Insurance Company)

A lifetime income annuity is also a great alternative to a low yielding CD. This illustration describes a time when CDs were still paying 1.75%. One couple, looking for a safe return, invested $100,000 in a CD. Even at 1.75% interest, their annual after-tax income was only $1,260 (about $100/ month) on a $100,000 investment. But feeling discouraged by their lack of income, they called their insurance agent asking how to improve their income. The agent said these exact words: "CDs were not made for income." That is what lifetime income annuities were made for. A joint lifetime income with cash refund annuity would guarantee this family 333% more income guaranteed for the rest of both of their lives and still protect their family in case of an early death of both of them (see chart above).

Take a look at this next chart. The gray line represents the payout rates of lifetime income annuities from 2005-2010. The CD rates are in black. Notice the difference – the lifetime income annuities will typically pay more than CDs. Why? Because unlike CDs, there are three components to an annuity paycheck. It is not just interest. It includes principal, interest, and mortality credits. It is really the mortality credits that distinguish lifetime income annuities from other financial products. Mortality credits are a financial reward that increases the longer you live.

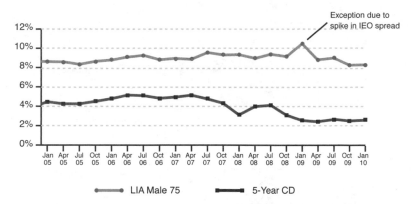

**Historical CD Interest Rates & Lifetime Income Annuity
Payout Rates 2005-2010 by Quarter**

Source: New York Life Insurance Company

Still, some may opt for a CD or money market investment because they believe interest rates will soar sometime
soon. As previously discussed, that may or may not happen,
but let's say the rates actually do climb. Did you know that
some insurance companies now offer a feature that raises
your monthly paycheck if the company sees interest rates
beginning to rise? The New York Life Lifetime Income Annuity
provides a good example of this feature. Under its current
Income Enhancement Option, if interest rates go up 2% or
more over the next five years, your annuity paycheck would
go up approximately 21% for the remainder of your life. Ask
your financial advisor if they have an annuity option like this
– many of them do.

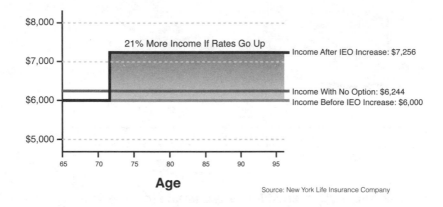

Source: New York Life Insurance Company

Leaving a Legacy: How Never to Be Forgotten

Why do grandparents and grandchildren get along so well? Because they have a common enemy – or so the old joke goes. But all kidding aside, most grandparents do want to leave some sort of legacy to their grandchildren. How about a guaranteed lifetime payment for both you and your grandchildren?

I remember once I was setting up a retirement plan for a 70-year-old client. He said, "I've got this beautiful 5-year-old granddaughter. I want to do something special for her. Now, some people say I should buy life insurance, but others say I shouldn't. Some people say I should put it in a 529 college savings plan, and again, some others say I shouldn't. Do you have any ideas?"

I said, "Yes, I've got some ideas. But before I give you my ideas, I've got to prove a point." I handed him a piece of paper and on this piece of paper there were four lines on the top and eight lines on the bottom. I said, "On these top four lines, do me a favor – jot down the first and last names of your four grandparents – grandma and grandpa on your mom's side, grandma and grandpa on your dad's side. Their first and last names. Everybody can do it."

On average, only about half of everyone reading this book can list the first and last names of all four of their grandparents. Isn't that amazing? Then I said, "On these eight lines, do me a favor – jot down the first and last names of your eight great-grandparents. Go ahead, it should just take a minute. I'll wait." Needless to say, I have never been on an appointment where somebody could remember the first and last names of their eight great-grandparents.

"You know what's so interesting about that?" I continued, "John D. Rockefeller's great-great-great-grandkids all remember his first and last name. How could John D. Rockefeller's great-great-great-grandkids remember him while you don't even remember grandma and grandpa? Well, it's because every year they get a check from John D. Rockefeller." John D. Rockefeller always said to leave something behind, and that he most definitely did.

My recommendation was to set up a joint lifetime annuity between the grandpa and his 5-year-old granddaughter. I told him: "To make this even more special, we will ask the insurance company to make the payment each year on your granddaughter's birthday. For the rest of your life, every time she has a birthday, you're going to get a check from the insurance company and you can use that to put in a life insurance policy. You can put it in a 529 plan. You could buy her a pony. If she turns out the way you don't like, you can spend it. But, for the rest of your life, every time she has a birthday, you're going to get a check from the insurance company. But," I said, "starting from the day you die, that beautiful granddaughter is going to get a present from her *favorite* grandpa every birthday for the rest of her life. She's never going to forget you. She's going to remember you on line number one, just like John D. Rockefeller. And on the day that your granddaughter dies, your great-granddaughter is going to get half of all the money you ever put in this account. She'll get it income tax-free. She's going to remember you right there on line number one as well."

Here is how it works in practice. You have a generous grandpa. He possesses $100,000 of lazy money. He buys a joint life (with a 50% death benefit) lifetime income annuity. The joint annuitant is his 5-year-old granddaughter. For the rest of his life, he gets $4,700 every year that she has a birthday (again, these payout rates can change, so check with your financial advisor for an updated quote). When grandpa dies, she continues to get a birthday present of $4,700 every birthday for the rest of her life. Let me pause right there. If you had a grandparent who gave you $4,700 every birthday for your entire life, would you remember him or her? I think so. And on the day that the granddaughter dies, the great-granddaughter will receive half of the original deposit: $50,000 income, tax-free. If you had a great-grandma or great-grandpa who left you $50,000 income tax-free, don't you think that might separate them from the pack a little bit?

You may be wondering, "What about inflation?" With an annuity, you can also purchase an inflation protection rider. You can add a 5% inflation factor on it. The first birthday present goes down to $1,100, but every year that goes up by 5%. When she is 20, it is $2,400. When she is 50, it is $10,700.

When she is 65, it is $22,000. Now if the granddaughter lives to be 100, which by the way is a distinct possibility, she will get paid $2,563,000 plus the $50,000 death benefit, a total payout on that original $100,000 investment of $2.6 million. Where else can a grandpa take $100,000, be guaranteed that two generations of his family will never forget his name, and out of that $100,000 transfer potentially $2.6 million? That grandparent could be you!

Annuity with Inflation Protection

Granddaughter's Age	Annual Birthday Present
1	$1,100
20	$2,400
50	$10,700
65	$22,000
Death Benefit	$50,000

* Note: Utilizing a joint life annuity to leave a legacy could have gift, estate, and generation skipping (GST) tax consequences. It is important, therefore, to consult with a qualified professional so that you reduce or eliminate any potential tax liabilities if you choose to pursue this strategy. These are sample payment rates, actual rates will vary.

(Source: New York Life Insurance Company)

Customized Solutions to Everyday Retirement Problems

 Key Points from Chapter 4

1. You can generate a hassle-free guaranteed income for life by using a lifetime income annuity to satisfy your RMDs. If you are married, consider using a joint life with cash refund option. Remember, you don't owe your kids a nickel of your IRA or 401(k) money – you saved that for *your* retirement!

2. In general, the breadwinner should delay taking Social Security – until age 70 if possible, since that Social Security check will cover both lives.

3. Many seniors can reduce or eliminate taxes on their Social Security benefits by using annuities properly. Many don't realize that all tax-free bond interest *counts* toward the taxation of their Social Security benefits.

4. Everyone should consider converting their IRA to a Roth IRA since it is possible to "un-convert" if necessary. Note that you must follow the IRS guidelines when it comes to

recharacterizing your Roth IRA back to regular IRA.

5. For people in their seventies who have lost money in the market, using a joint life with 30 years certain lifetime income annuity to help get back much or all of what was lost may make sense.

6. CDs weren't made for income – that is what a lifetime income annuity was made for!

7. You can have generations of your family remember your name, just like John D. Rockefeller. Use a joint lifetime income annuity with 50% death benefit to create a multi-generational payout system.

Chapter 5

Annuities: Insure Your Investments

I am always amazed at the reactions I receive from people when I use the word "annuity." Some people absolutely love annuities. Some people hate annuities. Some think they know exactly what an annuity is because their grandmother receives $435 every month from Prudential. Others are wary of annuities because they do not understand them.

This chapter will try to clear up any misconceptions you might have about annuities. The truth is, any product on its own is neither good nor bad. Considering what the product does, what the product is, and how the product is used will help you understand annuities more clearly and decide if it may make sense for you. Annuities are really risk management tools. You can transfer many of the retirement risks we have discussed to an insurance company. Market risk, longevity risk, inflation risk, deflation risk, order of returns risk, and withdrawal rate risk can all be transferred to an insurance company. You can, in fact, insure your investments. Annuities can do things that no other product in the world can do. But if that is true, why do so many people hate annuities? It is not that annuities are bad, but rather that there are bad annuities. Unfortunately, too many people have been affected by bad annuities or know someone who has. This has led some people to simply declare that all annuities are bad. That is simply not true. (Later in this chapter, the differences between good and bad annuities will be explored more closely.)

In the meantime, it is necessary to understand annuities in general. Annuities are purchased through insurance companies. There are thousands of annuities in the marketplace today, but based on their payout strategies, all of these annuities can be separated into two broad categories: immediate annuities and deferred annuities. That's it. There are no other choices. So let's take a look at both.

Immediate Annuities

An immediate annuity works when a lump sum is paid to an insurance company. Normally, payments begin immediately or within 12 months. I say normally because as I write this book, there are a couple of companies who allow you to now defer that income up to 40 years! An immediate annuity's primary purpose is to provide guaranteed income. This income can either be guaranteed for a period of time (fixed period annuities) or for your entire life (lifetime income annuities).

Fixed Period Annuities

A fixed period annuity is a type of immediate annuity that

pays a guaranteed income for a fixed period of time (for example, 5, 10, or 20 years). This annuity provides a certain amount of income for a specified period of time. It can be used in real estate transactions or to pay annual obligations like life insurance premiums over a period of time. Once that time is over, the payments stop and there is no more money in the annuity. It has completely paid out. Each paycheck from a fixed period annuity contains both principal and interest. No mortality credits are paid in a fixed period annuity.

Fixed period annuities are more popular when interest rates are high, as they were in the 1970s and 1980s. Recently, however, fixed period annuities have been less attractive because of today's low interest rate environment. Fixed period annuities have no fees or charges – they are a spread product, which means the insurance company has to make more money than what they are paying you in order to make a profit. Any "loads" are part of the pricing of the product. You will know exactly how much you will receive for the stated period of time and premium you give them.

Lifetime Income Annuities

The second type of immediate annuity is a lifetime income annuity. Some people know it as a single premium immediate annuity, or SPIA. This book has focused on this type of annuity because you simply cannot retire properly without one. As we discussed earlier, a lifetime income annuity is a guaranteed paycheck for life. Both qualified (IRA or 401(k)) and non-qualified money can be used in these annuities. Some popular examples are Social Security and company pensions

– these are actually lifetime income annuities.

Lifetime income annuities have many different options which make them flexible and allow you to make significant decisions based on what is best for you and your beneficiaries. The income can be based on one life or two lives. The two lives can be any two people – husband and wife, father and son, even two golfing buddies. This product also works well with same-sex couples. A joint lifetime income annuity between husband and wife, for example, means that if you pass away and your spouse remains alive, payments will continue for the remainder of your spouse's life. Different guarantee options are available: you can choose no guarantee beyond your life, or you can have your initial premium minus the payments received guaranteed to your beneficiaries, which would be paid to them in a cash refund, a lump sum, or installment payments. You can also have life with period certain guaranteed. This option will pay you for the rest of your life, but if you die prematurely, it will continue the payments for a period of time. There are also some companies that have life with a guaranteed death benefit of 25% or 50% of the original premium.

If all of this seems confusing, it really isn't. When you get an illustration from your financial or insurance professional, all of these options will be listed and the payout rate will be different for each one. So which choice is best? That is totally up to you. Neither the insurance company nor your financial or insurance professional has a financial incentive to push one option over the other. This decision depends on what is most important to you and your family, your health, and your best guess at your life expectancy. Sometimes people take out more than one annuity with different guarantees to maximize potential benefits.

Only about 8% of all lifetime income annuities take the life only option (according to a Major Life Insurance Company's experience). So 92% of all lifetime income annuity buyers want a guarantee in case of their premature death. When I really started getting involved with lifetime income annuities in the early 2000s, I was a big fan of life with cash refund. It certainly is the easiest to explain and understand. If you give the insurance company $100,000 and they guarantee to pay you $10,000 per year, and you die after two years, your family gets the remaining $80,000. On the other hand, if you live for 20 years, the insurance company has to pay you a total of $200,000. That is a very simple proposition, and simple is usually best.

However, the more I have studied these products and the research surrounding them, the more I am a believer in life only or joint life only. This is where you maximize the benefits of mortality credits. In fact, when it comes time for me to buy my lifetime income annuities, that is my plan – to buy joint life payouts for my wife and me. We will leave our kids other assets. In fact, by using life only, the research shows you will probably be able to leave your children more money. So while everyone buys guarantees just in case they die early, at least half of these people – probably closer to 65% – would be better off taking a life only contract.

WITHDRAWAL RIGHTS

Many people believe that lifetime income annuities are illiquid investments, meaning that the principal is untouchable outside of scheduled payments. For example, you cannot go to the Social Security Administration and ask for a $50,000 withdrawal from your future Social Security benefits. How-ever, with your lifetime income annuity, you could walk into a number of life insurance companies and ask for a withdrawal of a lump sum. Each company handles withdrawals differ-ently, so you will want to ask for specifics.

Generally, the insurance company would take the amount of guaranteed payments you have remaining and apply a calculation to determine what amount of withdrawal is pos-sible. One specific insurance carrier, for example, offers an annuity with a very attractive feature where if a client makes a 100% cash withdrawal, and the client remains alive after the guaranteed period, payments would resume for the rest of the client's life as if no withdrawal had been made. Some other companies terminate the annuity once a 100% with-drawal has been made. Others offer payment acceleration features that allow you to get the next six payments or more in a lump sum. Normally, payments would stop until after those payments have been made, and then future payments would resume as scheduled. So a number of lifetime income annuities offer more flexibility than most people think.

PAYMENT OPTIONS

Insurance companies are becoming very helpful in address-ing client objections to lifetime income annuities. We just discussed how many have incorporated guarantees and withdrawal privileges into their annuities. Other features are continually being incorporated into annuity plans from many companies.

How about flexibility in payment amounts? Some people would like to have larger checks initially while waiting for Social Security or pension income to start, then have lower annuity checks once these other sources of income begin. Others would rather have lower paychecks from their annuity now, while a business or real estate sale is providing them income, but want larger checks in the future when these payments stop. These options offer tremendous flexibility as your needs change and are available from some insurance companies today.

A new option provides flexibility in payment timing. There are a couple of companies who now allow you to defer taking income from an annuity for 5, 10, 20, even 40 years in exchange for a higher payout rate. This new type of annuity is called a deferred income annuity, although it falls under the immediate annuity umbrella. The payout rates of these products are very compelling. For example, someone in their mid-50s who wants income at age 65 could have guaranteed payout rates of 11%. Someone age 65 who wants to start income at age 85 as a form of "longevity insurance" could very well receive a guaranteed payout rate near 70%!

INFLATION PROTECTION

Many lifetime income annuities offer inflation protection. You can have your paycheck go up by 1%, 2%, or even up to 5% per year. Naturally, your initial paycheck will be lower or you will have to put more money in to keep payment amounts constant over time. Less than 4% of all lifetime income annuities sold have inflation protection on them. Why so low? Perhaps because the initial paycheck amount drops significantly with inflation protection. Also, as people age into their eighties and nineties, they tend to spend less and less each year, which can serve as a form of unofficial inflation protection. A big exception here would be all of the seniors who did not purchase long-term care insurance. Many of those people will likely end up spending most or all of their money on end-of-life care.

A strategy that offers inflation protection with maximum flexibility is to ladder your lifetime income annuity purchases. That just means you do not have to spend all of your money on a lifetime income annuity. You can buy one that covers your basic expenses and invest the rest of your money with an eye on inflation. Stocks and commodities, for example, are sensitive to inflation. If inflation goes up, these investments should rise as well. You can take some of those profits to buy another lifetime income annuity later on to give your income inflation protection as well. Repeat as necessary throughout your retirement. This keeps more of your money liquid while still protecting you from an inflationary environment.

Another feature some insurance companies have added will raise your paycheck if interest rates rise. Normally, if interest rates go up 2% over five years, for example, the income from your annuity is raised by about 21%. Again, each company is different, so ask about this feature to enhance income potential. Another way to protect against inflation is to purchase a variable immediate annuity. These are lifetime income annuities that give you a monthly paycheck which can fluctuate based on the market value of the underlying investment options that the annuity has been invested in. Variable immediate annuities are just a sliver of the income annuity market, and only a few companies even offer them. However, not all baby boomers are going to want fixed interest type products, especially as some of these variable immediate annuities come with guaranteed floors to reduce overall market risk on the variable investment options.

I am not going to go into detail on these products, but basically they use an Assumed Interest Rate (AIR), normally in the 3% to 6% range, to calculate the initial payouts. Each year, a recalculation is done and the payout is adjusted. If the investments do better, an upward adjustment is made. If the investments do worse, a downward adjustment is made. Again, some of these have a guaranteed minimum floor so that the payments will not go lower than a certain amount. Over the long term, these annuities have the potential to pay more than the guaranteed version of a fixed lifetime income annuity but with risk exposure to principle. Variable annuities are offered via a prospectus so be sure to call your financial professional for the prospectus applicable to any one you may consider purchasing and read it carefully for the specific applicable fees, expense and risk factors. So keep your eye on these products – you will be seeing more of them in the future.

 Longevity Insurance

Another form of a lifetime income annuity is called longevity insurance. Think of this type of annuity as the opposite of term life insurance. Both term life insurance and longevity insurance are very inexpensive. Term life insurance only pays if you die. Longevity insurance only pays if you live. A 65 year old could take 10%-15% of his portfolio value and buy longevity insurance with a very high payout rate (65%-75%) each year for the rest of his life starting at age 85. That means the other 85%-90% of his portfolio would be liquid and would only need to last to age 85.

It is technically a deferred income annuity because annuitization (taking income payments) would be delayed until age 85, but payments would be very high. Longevity insurance is really taking all of the mortality credits we talked about earlier and maximizing their use at the end of your life. It is a more sophisticated strategy for keeping as much control over your investments as possible while taking full advantage of the mortality credits that only a lifetime income annuity can provide.

FEES AND TAXES

Just like a fixed period annuity, a lifetime income annuity is a spread product and normally has no annual fees and charges. Many will have a $150 to $300 one-time policy fee, but that amount has already been calculated in the payout rate. Again, you will know exactly how much per month you will receive based on the amount you give the insurance company. One huge benefit of the lifetime income annuity is the taxation of the payments. For non-qualified money (outside of an IRA or 401(k)), only a portion of the monthly payment is taxable. Remember, each paycheck consists of principal, interest, and mortality credits. The principal is not taxable. For example, $12,000 of annual income from a lifetime income annuity may only result in $3,000-$4,000 of taxable income! This amount will be shown on the illustration you receive from your financial advisor. Remember that once your entire principal has been paid back to you, all of the remaining payments will be fully taxable. Qualified money is fully taxable as well.

Deferred Annuities

The deferred annuity is a type of annuity used for saving and investing. In contrast to the immediate annuity, deferred annuities do not begin payments right away, but rather allow your money to grow over time. An advantage of deferred annuities is that while your money is growing, and before payments begin, there are no taxes to be paid. The only time you have a taxable event in a deferred annuity is when you make a withdrawal (or in a change of ownership where the IRS considers you to have constructive receipt). But while the money is growing in the deferred annuity, no taxes are due. In this respect, deferred annuities are similar to a traditional IRA.

Another advantage of a deferred annuity is that it can be turned into income at any time. There are two ways to do this. First, you can annuitize the contract. This annuitization literally turns a deferred annuity into a lifetime income annuity. Annuitization is the process of collecting income from your annuity, so annuitization in a deferred annuity would not happen until payments started. Many annuities also offer the option to turn income on and off. This is called a systematic withdrawal. You can determine what amount you want per month. This amount can be changed or stopped at any time. For example, if you begin collecting payments and then sell your house, you can put payments on hold and live off the lump sum from the house sale. This way the principal in your annuity continues to collect interest and grow. Just make sure that when you make withdrawals, they do not violate the withdrawal terms of your annuity and subject you to unnecessary surrender charges and/or tax penalties.

If you annuitize the contract, understand that payout rates vary, so you would want to compare the annuitization payout rate offered by the deferred annuity versus the payout rate from a new lifetime income annuity when you are ready to start collecting your paycheck. Some companies use a higher rate for their new lifetime income annuities than the annuitization rate from their deferred annuities.

Why would these differences exist? Possibly because many people have no idea how these contracts work, and it is easier to just annuitize an existing contract than to shop around for higher payout rates. Insurance companies know this, so often they can get away with paying a lower rate for annuitized deferred contracts. Payout rates for annuitized contracts also carry a higher risk for insurance companies, because they can only change them once each year (for lifetime income annuities, rates can change every two weeks but are fixed at the time of purchase). A good financial advisor would know this and should steer you the right way. Deferred annuities also offer guarantees which are discussed below that are not offered by other products.

Fixed Deferred Annuities

Like immediate annuities, there are two types of deferred annuities – fixed and variable. A fixed deferred annuity is the
insurance company's version of a Certificate of Deposit or
CD (although fixed annuities are not FDIC-insured). Every
day, the value of a fixed deferred annuity goes up. Typically,
fixed deferred annuities pay a higher rate of interest than
CDs. Another huge plus is that there are no taxes due until a
withdrawal is made! Compare that to a CD, where taxes are
due on the interest each and every year – even if you never
touch the interest! If you are looking for a fixed annuity, here
is some advice that will keep you out of trouble. First, look
for the highest rated insurance companies, then compare the
interest rates offered from these highly rated carriers. Finally,
look for a money-back guarantee at any time just in case you
change your mind or have some type of emergency. If you
follow those simple rules, you will never be burned by a fixed
deferred annuity.

Just like fixed immediate annuities, fixed deferred annuities are spread products, so there are normally no annual
fees. You will get exactly the interest rate that they declare.
Remember, however, this is an annual interest rate. There
is no daily or weekly compounding of interest. It is compounded annually. In addition, fixed deferred annuities do
have surrender charges (similar to an early withdrawal penalty). Typically they are 6%-8% of the initial premium and
phase out over a 5-8 year period. Be very cautious of any
fixed annuity that has higher or longer surrender charges,
which means that insurance companies can assess a fee if
you withdraw money within a time frame (often six to eight
years after depositing the principal). Most companies allow

a 10% penalty-free withdrawal each year, but check your contract. Remember, surrender charges are not necessarily bad – they allow an insurance company to pay you a higher interest rate because they know that money will be "sticky" and will not be going anywhere for a while. You just do not want an annuity with surrender charges that are excessively high or excessively long.

Another thing to look for is a money-back guarantee at any time. A handful of highly-rated companies offer a money-back guarantee on their fixed annuities. That does not mean they don't have a surrender charge – it simply means the surrender charge will never touch your principal. You may have to forfeit your interest in case of an early withdrawal, but you won't have to lose any of your principal. It is absolutely worth looking for this type of guarantee.

Some fixed annuities are single premium while others are flexible premium. Flexible premium simply means you can add money to the contract – normally at any time, subject to a minimum deposit amount. Check the contract to see how yours works.

Fixed Index Annuity

One type of fixed deferred annuity is a fixed index annuity. This is a fixed annuity that does not declare a specific interest rate up front. Instead, it uses a formula based on the performance of an index – the most popular being the S&P 500 stock index. But I have seen real estate indices, commodities, and many other indices used. There are financial advisors who swear by these annuities. I have spoken at meetings where index annuity guru Jack Marion has eloquently explained the advantages of these products. If you are interested in learning more about fixed index annuities, visit Jack's website at www.indexannuity.org.

ARE FIXED INDEX ANNUITIES REALLY A GOOD INVESTMENT?

In the past (even in earlier editions of this book), I have been very skeptical of index annuities. I had seen many of these products over-promise and under deliver. I just believed there were superior products to accomplish what these products said they would do for you.

However, these products have performed admirably over the past decade. Some of the "gotcha's" have been removed and even the major companies are taking a second look. Some of these products now have some outstanding income guarantees. When you combine those guarantees with some of the guaranteed roll up numbers, they may play a key role for some retirees in the income planning phase.

These products have so many bells and whistles that I do believe it is important to deal with a trustworthy and competent financial professional. Stick with the highest rated companies and compare the income you could get from the guarantees offered from these fixed index annuities to the guaranteed income you could receive from a Lifetime Income Annuity. I think what you will find is that some younger ages may do better with the Fixed Index Annuity and older ages will do better with the Lifetime Income Annuity.

Deferred Variable Annuity

That leads me to the final type of deferred annuity – the variable annuity. This is the most popular type of annuity in the entire insurance industry based on LIMRA's 2010 U.S. Individual Annuities Sales Survey. In 2010, sales of variable annuities reached $140.5 billion according to *Insurance & Financial Advisor News* (Feb. 16, 2011). These are also the annuities that many so-called financial experts in the media have labeled "rip-offs." Why are these products so popular with financial advisors and the public but, at the same time, so hated by the media and so-called financial experts? Ben Bernanke, the Chairman of the Federal Reserve, had much of his money invested in variable annuities according to an August 2, 2010 *Wall Street Journal* report. Ben Stein, who you might watch each Saturday morning on the Fox Business Network, is a believer in variable annuities as well. John Huggard, J.D., CFP is a full-time professor, an Alumni

Distinguished Professor, and is a member of the Academy of Outstanding Teachers at North Carolina State University. He wrote a book on variable annuities called *Investing with Variable Annuities: Fifty Reasons Why Variable Annuities Are Better Long Term Investments Than Mutual Funds*. If you are a variable annuity non-believer, I would strongly encourage you to read this book.

Without delving too extensively into variable deferred annuities, there are certainly some practical, real-world reasons for considering these annuities. This is money that you are using to grow for retirement; if you are already retired, you can use this money to optimize your portfolio. So what is a variable deferred annuity? It is simply a deferred annuity that allows you to invest in the market on a tax-deferred basis. The average variable annuity will offer 20 to 50 different portfolios (called investment divisions or subaccounts), but some annuities may offer a hundred or more. Since most individuals will probably only choose 6 to 10 investment options, the quantity of investment options available is not as important as the quality. Also, variable annuities have no caps or limits on how much the funds can go up.

VARIABLE ANNUITY GUARANTEES

These annuities do offer some guarantees to protect you and your family from significant market risk. First, variable annuities come with a guaranteed death benefit. This protects your family and beneficiaries from any market loss should you die when the value of the annuity is worth less than your initial investment. For example, if you put $100,000 into a variable annuity but died when the account value was down to $75,000 due to a drop in the market, your family would receive the $100,000 as a guaranteed death benefit.

Many variable annuities also have a reset provision that allows an increase in the death benefit guarantee. The most common is an annual reset on the anniversary of purchase. For example, if you put $100,000 in a variable annuity with an annual reset death benefit, and on the third anniversary the account value was $140,000, the guaranteed minimum death benefit would then step up to $140,000. If market losses then caused the annuity to drop to $110,000 and you died, your family would receive the $140,000 death benefit. There have been countless families who could tell you their own stories about what a great benefit this has been for them. There may be an additional fee for this benefit.

In addition to guaranteed death benefits, variable annuities can also offer guaranteed living benefits. These are guarantees for you while you are still alive. They really come in three major forms: Guaranteed Minimum Income Benefit Riders (GMIB), Guaranteed Minimum Withdrawal Benefit Riders (GMWB), and Guaranteed Minimum Accumulation Benefit Riders (GMAB). My favorite is the Guaranteed Minimum Accumulation Benefit Rider – mainly because it is a cash value guarantee. That will be discussed at the end of this chapter, so let's focus on the other two – GMIBs and GMWBs. Both of these riders have been much more popular than the GMAB not necessarily because they are better, but because more companies offer them and they appear to have more sizzle.

GUARANTEED MINIMUM INCOME BENEFIT RIDERS (GMIB)

A GMIB rider guarantees that no matter what the market does, the client will be guaranteed a minimum income for life. So, if the market goes up, your account value will go up and you can draw income off of this investment like you could from any investment. However, if the market goes down, you are guaranteed an income based on the original amount invested. Often there are step-up or roll-up guarantees of 5% to 7% that would also apply in such a circumstance. An important thing to remember in a GMIB contract is that you must annuitize the contract (start taking income) to receive that guarantee.

This whole book has been about the importance of annuitizing assets in retirement, so this would be a great product, right? Not necessarily. To give this guarantee, the insurance company cannot give you the same annuitization (payout) rates as a fixed lifetime income annuity. Most of these contracts reduce the rate by an amount similar to subtracting 10 years from your age at the time of purchase. So, the annuitization rate in a variable annuity with a GMIB for a 70-year-old would be similar to the payout of a 60-year-old buying a lifetime income annuity. This reduction often wipes out the guaranteed growth of 6% that many of these contracts offered.

However, it is still a better guarantee than you would have in a mutual fund or individual stocks and bonds. If you choose this type of contract, the most important thing is to look at the financial strength of the issuing company. In the 2008-2009 market crash, we saw people who had purchased this type of contract with plummeting account values. They wanted to use their guarantee, but their insurance company may have been downgraded several times and was experiencing serious financial difficulties. At that point, people either had to take a large loss and move to a stronger carrier and lock in a lower amount of income, or receive the higher guaranteed income, giving up all liquidity, and be tied to a company for the rest of their lives which may not be financially sound. One should avoid getting into a situation like that in retirement. Stick to the highest-rated carriers regardless of what type of annuity you buy.

GUARANTEED MINIMUM WITHDRAWAL BENEFIT RIDERS (GMWB)

The second, and now more popular, type of guarantee is the Guaranteed Minimum Withdrawal Benefit rider. This contract gives more flexibility than the GMIB contract in that you do not have to annuitize the contract to get income. Again, if the market is up, the GMWB contract has the same income options that almost any other similar investment would have. However, in a down market, you have a minimum withdrawal amount that is guaranteed for life.

Most of these contracts also guarantee a minimum roll-up factor of 4%-7%. Many people buying these contracts believe that their principal is guaranteed to grow by a certain percentage, say 6%, each year. If the market goes up, they get the upside of the market. But if the market falls, they think their cash value will go up by 6%. That is not true. These contracts have two values – the cash value and the benefit base value. The cash value goes up and down with the market, so guaranteed growth does not apply to this value. The benefit base, however, is guaranteed to grow by a minimum rate. There may also be a reset provision to the benefit base if the market goes up by more than the annual guarantee.

Investors need to know that the benefit base is not the principal. You cannot take all of that money out. When you die, it normally will not go to your family unless you purchase a separate rider. It is simply used to calculate your withdrawal benefit (normally 3% to 5% of the benefit base). While these GMWB riders certainly can provide income, they were really not meant for income; they are simply a guarantee that can help give you confidence to stay in the market during turbulent times. If the market does well, you will probably be much better off transferring into a lifetime income annuity and receiving a higher income after the surrender period on the variable annuity is expired.

The main problem with this type of variable annuity is that the fees can get very high – 4% or more in some cases. Your principal could very well run out in this type of annuity. However, your income is guaranteed for life as long as you do not violate any other provisions of the contract. Just be careful to clearly understand what you are buying. A great website that many financial advisors use to keep up-to-date on all of these variable annuities is www.advisorone.com. One feature on this site that I really like is that a good friend, Dr. Moshe Milevsky, has reviewed many of the variable annuities on the market, and grades each one. You can read what the pluses and minuses are for each contract and determine which one may be most appropriate for your specific situation. I have found this feature to be very helpful.

123 Fees – By the Numbers

There are four simple questions you should ask your financial professional or advisor before ever investing a penny into anything.

1. Is there a front end load?

Front loads are charges or commissions assessed at the time of investment; the fee is deducted from your investment amount, thereby lowering the total principal. Annuities typically have no front load.

2. Is there any type of policy fee or annual maintenance fee?

Most fixed annuities will not have these, although some will charge a fee for smaller accounts. Variable annuities may charge a fee for smaller accounts and will charge a fee for guaranteed living benefits and the reset death benefit rider.

3. Are there any hidden charges?

Not with fixed or lifetime income annuities. However, in variable annuities you will have a mortality and expense charge (which covers the death benefit and some of the other features) of anywhere from about 1% to 1.85% annually. Additionally, there is an annual fund fee on these accounts; such fees range from .4% to over 2%, but the average is 1%.

4. Are there any surrender charges and what are they?

Surrender charges are fees assessed if you

withdraw funds from your account before an agreed-upon date; the "surrender period" must pass before you can withdraw without this charge. These fees will normally range from 0% to 8% depending on how long you have held the annuity at withdrawal. Surrender periods are usually five to eight years, at which time the charges will be eliminated, but some annuities can have much longer surrender periods. I would avoid annuities with high surrender fees or long surrender periods. On the bright side, you can buy annuities with no surrender charge at all. As you would expect, they do not offer the same level of features or guarantees either.

Variable annuities have their detractors. There are three basic arguments against variable annuities that have become quite common.

1. Variable annuities have high fees.

2. Variable annuities are taxed at ordinary income rates rather than capital gains tax rates (on stocks, etc.).

3. Unlike stocks or mutual funds, annuities do not get a stepped-up cost basis at death. Stepping up the cost basis means that the valuation of an asset is locked in at the time of the investor's death for purposes of calculating the capital gains tax when the asset is ul-

timately sold. Annuities do not offer this tax benefit, which means that the grandkids may have to pay more taxes on their inherited funds.

Each of these arguments can easily be addressed using what this chapter has shown about annuities. First of all, high fees: there are many investment products with higher fees than annuities that do not provide the same value. There are countless cases of people who invested in the stock market, making low fee investments without guarantees, and lost entire fortunes. Many annuities offer guarantees that protect your principal, generally through riders for an additional fee. They also provide a minimum guaranteed death benefit. Those guarantees offer significant value. Because some variable annuities can protect your assets from downside risk, it is possible for the average person to confidently make a significant investment that offers the potential upside of the market with some limited risk exposure.

Secondly, variable annuities make you pay ordinary income tax rates on gains instead of the lower capital gains tax rates. The higher tax rate on annuity income may seem problematic. However, only stocks held for over a year get capital gains tax breaks, and mutual fund turnover rates are so high that very few actually benefit from these tax breaks.

Finally, there is the cost basis argument. If you choose to invest in stocks, it is possible that your heirs might benefit from a stepped-up cost basis. For example, if someone buys Intel stock at $10 per share and holds it for 20 years, the value of the stock might increase to $25. This $15 difference between the original price ($10) and the $25 is called the capital gain. If this person sells the stock at this point, he or she will have to pay taxes on the $15 per share capital gain (long-term capital gains tax is normally about 15%).

On the other hand, if our investor held onto the stock until he or she died and passed it on to his or her grandchildren, they would inherit the stock at its current value and the new cost basis would be $25 (the price upon their inheritance). Their cost basis would be $25 instead of $10. If the grand-children sold it a year later for $27, they would save money on taxes because the capital gain would only be $2 per share.

This tax benefit from inheriting securities is called a step-up in cost basis. While annuities do not get that stepped-up cost basis at death, it should also be noted that annuities do not get a stepped-down cost basis at death either. Think of all of the investments that went down over the last decade. When the investor died, their family received far less than what had been originally invested. With an annuity, the guar-anteed death benefit would have protected the family from losing money at death.

Mutual funds also offer a stepped-up cost basis, but again, due to the high turnover of many of these funds, inves-tors also have to pay taxes annually on any fund distributions. You may have experienced this situation in recent years when your mutual funds declined and you still owed a tax. In this way, investors are actually paying for the stepped-up cost basis in taxes. The only free stepped-up cost basis at death is on unrealized capital gains. Additionally, a number of an-nuities offer a rider that will pay most or all of the taxes due upon death. These riders come at additional cost, but if taxes are truly your concern, the rider can eliminate that worry.

Exits and Transfers

There is some amount of confusion on transferring annuities from one company to another, but it is actually quite simple. First of all, if you have IRA money, the annuity would really be no different than any other IRA. You could directly transfer your IRA, or actually take possession of the money for up to 60 days before opening a new IRA. (The IRS gives you 60 days to make the transfer.) Some simple advice: check for any surrender penalties from the insurance company before moving any money, and do not push the 60-day limit. Most companies take a day or two or three to process the money. You do not want to have an unnecessary IRS problem because you pushed the 60-day limit. You can also do a qualified rollover from 401(k)s, 403(b)s, 457s, and other qualified plans into an IRA.

For non-qualified (non-IRA) money, you are allowed to do something called a 1035 exchange. A 1035 exchange allows you to make transfers that are not taxable events: one can transfer a life insurance policy to another life insurance policy, a life insurance policy into any type of annuity policy, or an annuity policy into any other annuity policy. "Non-taxable event" doesn't mean taxes will never be due, but that the original cost basis will transfer to the new contract and tax deferral will continue. A 1035 exchange allows you, as the investor, to pursue better opportunities in different kinds of accounts without paying a tax on the transfer and gives you more control over your funds.

A few words of caution: these exchanges are also one of the most abused privileges in the insurance industry. Ensure that your transfer is going to benefit you; sometimes the original policy might very well have higher guaranteed interest rates, higher reset death benefits, or lower fees. Spend time researching your investments on the front-end and you will not have regrets on the back-end.

 ## BAD ANNUITIES

What is a bad annuity? I like to put it this way: in military intelligence, it is impossible to pinpoint the details of an enemy attack. Instead of attempting to predict the unknowable, it becomes important to recognize when the enemy might be preparing for an attack (for example, stockpiling supplies or amassing troops). All those signs are called "indicators and warnings."

So instead of attempting to pinpoint bad annuities, it is important to learn the indicators and warnings of bad annuities.

INDICATOR 1: Bad annuities typically have high surrender charges. Surrender charges are fees assessed by the insurance company if you withdraw your funds prematurely; a charge over 8% is likely to be suspect.

INDICATOR 2: Bad annuities typically have long surrender charges. Surrender chargers can only be assessed during the surrender period; that is, after a certain time has passed since the initial investment, you can withdraw your money with no fee. This time should be eight years or less. A surrender period longer than that should generally be a warning sign.

INDICATOR 3: Forced annuitization of a deferred annuity is an indicator of a bad annuity. Annuitization describes the process by which income is distributed back to the investor. While all deferred annuities obviously offer annuitization as an option, some annuities require you to annuitize the contract or, if you die, require your children to annuitize the contract. You should be able to determine when to annuitize the contract yourself and raise a red flag if you are not allowed to decide.

INDICATOR 4: High commissions. Be wary of any annuity that pays the financial advisor more than 4%-6% in commissions. Additional indicators and warnings include surrender penalties at death, limited liquidity, or unusually high fees. While any one of these may not indicate a bad annuity, bad annuities typically have one or more of the above features. Remember, it is your money – take good care of it!

Dealing With Market Risk

Now that we have covered the mechanics and features of annuities, it is important to consider how they can help you limit market risk during these turbulent times. Dealing with market volatility and its impact on your retirement assets has been extremely difficult given the wild market gyrations of recent years. In general, there are three things a good financial advisor can do to help you tolerate market risk: one, they can help you manage market risk; two, they can help you put a floor under market risk; and three, they can help you eliminate market risk.

1. Managing Market Risk

First of all, when it comes to managing risk, I like to use the example of the 1987 stock market crash, one of the worst in the history of the U.S. stock market. This crash happened long enough ago that we can look at it now with a great deal of perspective. Looking at the chart below, you can see that the market crashed 23% in one day. For those of us who remember that day, the level of panic was something we had never seen before.

While rumors of stockbrokers jumping out of windows to commit suicide were proven to be false, there was still a widespread panic across the country that many of us had never experienced. The average investor had no idea what to do, and many sold just in time to lock in their losses (as the market soon regained its footing and continued to climb for decades).

The Market Correction in October 1987

Source: TomHegna.com and *The Wall Street Journal*

By putting risk into perspective, we can learn from the past and apply our knowledge to the future. As Warren Buffet said, "Buy when others are fearful, and be fearful when others are buying." The chart below shows the exact same 1987 stock market crash, but now in the framework of decades of stock market performance. Notice how, over the long term, those days of panic are merely blips amid the constant general upward climb of the market.

The Market in October 1987 through 2007

Source: TomHegna.com and *The Wall Street Journal*

As one major player put it:

On October 19, 1987, the Dow Jones Industrial Average fell approximately 23%, the second-largest one-day decline recorded in stock market history. Over the next 20 years, the Dow had multiple instances of significant short-term declines. For instance, in the summer of 1998, the Dow fell 17.11%; early on in 2000, the Dow fell 12.26%; in 2001, the Dow fell 20.09% over a four-month period; then over a six-month period in 2002 the Dow dropped more than 30%. Fortunately, during this 20-year period, the Dow has also risen almost 700% through December 31, 2007, passing 14,000 for the first time in trading on July 19. While historically, the Dow experienced significant declines on several occasions, but by adopting a long-term perspective, investors can put short-term events into perspective, lower the impact of market volatility, and realize positive results.

You will not need to panic about market volatility if you understand the key tenets to successful investing: invest for the long term, diversify your portfolio, and utilize proper asset allocation with regular rebalancing. Because of the lost decade of the 2000s in the stock market, many people say these tenets are dead, or that you have to day trade in order to make money. When it comes to day trading, here is my advice: if you want to make a small fortune in day trading, start with a large fortune. No one knows what the market is going to do, or when. No one. It is important to keep that in perspective.

2. Putting a Floor Under Market Risk

This leads me into my second point – putting a floor under market risk. What if you could have the upside of the market, but not the downside? You would probably be interested in this investment. Now let me ask you this: if such an investment existed, would you invest differently? If your normal asset allocation comprised 60% in stocks and 40% in bonds, would you dare go to 70% or even 80% in stocks? Would you now choose to put some money in commodities or currencies?

Well, such an investment truly does exist. It is called a variable annuity with a Guaranteed Minimum Accumulation Benefit rider. This investment allows you to choose your stock and/or bond funds, invest in the market, and capture the full upside of the market, but you are guaranteed not to lose a penny over a certain period of time – normally 10 years. These products also come with a guaranteed death benefit that protects your family from market losses upon your death. For example, suppose you invested $100,000 in a 10-year variable annuity with the Guaranteed Minimum Accumulation Benefit rider. You would be guaranteed to get your original $100,000 back at the end of the 10-year period even if your investments were worth less than that due to market losses. If you pass away during the 10-year period, the death benefit would provide your beneficiaries with at minimum the amount of your initial investment. While you have to pay a fee for these risk management provisions up front, it will insure that your investment never falls below what you started with.

Both of these guarantees can typically be stepped-up or reset on each policy anniversary up to a certain age (for instance, age 65 for qualified money and age 75 for non-qualified money). The step-up allows you to lock in gains and therefore will increase your guaranteed minimum accumulation benefit. For example, suppose you invested

$100,000 with an annual step-up. If after a year the value of your investment increased to $125,000, you could lock in the $125,000 as the new value of your guaranteed minimum accumulation benefit. This step-up means that you will be guaranteed at least the $125,000 10 years from your step-up date regardless of future market performance.

The media loves to attack variable annuities. One journalist even called them a "ripoff" in a *Forbes* article. In my seminars, I have challenged my audiences to show me any place in the world that I can invest my money that will give me more upside, with lower downside, after fees. A pretty simple challenge – more upside, lower downside after fees. And yet, after nearly 3,000 seminars in all 50 states, I have yet to be presented an alternative to my variable annuity that will satisfy those simple requirements.

While critics seem to focus on the fees, which are higher than no-load mutual funds, they always overlook the value of the product for many investors. I have been on thousands of appointments, and in nearly all of them, the client wanted to make as much as they could on their investment. If they can make 10%, 20%, 30%, or even 50%, they will take as much as the market will give them. I have never found anyone who wanted to put a cap on the upside of their investments. At the same time, however, they do not want to lose what they have already got. That is exactly what a variable annuity with a Guaranteed Minimum Accumulation Benefit rider will do for them.

As we discussed, variable annuities with guaranteed minimum withdrawal benefits are all the rage. These products also put a floor on risk but in a slightly different manner. They guarantee a minimum withdrawal amount that can be used for income in retirement. However, they do not guarantee the cash value. Also, many advisors think these are income-producing vehicles. While they can be, the truly sharp financial professional recognizes that these are, in fact, sub-optimal income producers. When income is actually needed, there are many better options (the lifetime income annuity certainly comes to mind). Their real value is giving the client some amount of guarantee on their investment, which gives them the confidence to stay in the market during turbulent times. Remember, the primary purpose of a variable annuity is growth – not income.

3. Eliminating Market Risk

The third option for market risk is to simply eliminate it. In my 25 years in the insurance and investment business, I have met plenty of people who have just had it with risk and the stock market. No matter how good of a salesperson I was, I would never be able to convince them to rejoin the market. I am sure you know people just like that, or perhaps you are one yourself. It's OK – there are many, many wealthy people who do not believe in taking risks with their savings and investments. The fact is that you do not have to take risks with your investments to have a successful retirement.

Fixed deferred annuities, as we discussed earlier, are products that guarantee both the principal and interest. You invest money in the annuity and agree not to withdraw it for a certain period of time. Not surprisingly, fixed deferred annuities tend to pay a higher rate of interest than CDs. Another huge plus is that they are tax-deferred so there are no taxes due until a withdrawal is made. Compare that to a CD, where taxes are due each year – even if you never touch the interest.

Other people focus on the FDIC insurance that protects CD buyers. Some buyers are even so diligent as to spread their CDs over many banks. There is even the CDARS – the Certificate of Deposit Account Registry Service – which will spread your CDs around to make sure each of them has an appropriate level of FDIC insurance. I always wonder if these people have actually researched FDIC insurance. I have. If you go to the FDIC website (www.fdic.gov), you can read up on the history of FDIC insurance. You will then learn that there is a very small amount of money backing up a huge number of CDs. In fact, there is not enough FDIC insurance to fully protect even one of the major banks – much less the entire banking industry.

If a client tells me that FDIC is important to them, in jest I tell them that we should look online and find the smallest, weakest banks in America to buy CDs from. The way I see it, if the economy starts spiraling downward, the smallest and weakest banks will fail first – and then you might have a shot at some of that FDIC money.

Seriously, a far better option would be to look at the fixed deferred annuities offered by top-rated insurance companies. Of course, another great way to eliminate market risk is to buy a lifetime income annuity. As we have talked about (and will continue to talk about), a lifetime income annuity is a guaranteed paycheck for life – a lifetime of paychecks with an incredibly attractive payout rate and no market risk. This is truly a product meant to help you have a happy and successful retirement. So there you have it – if you are going to be in the market, manage your risk or put a floor under it. But keep in mind that you do not have to be in the market if you feel it is just not right for you.

ANNUITY TIMELINE – THEY ARE OLDER THAN YOU THINK

AD 225

AD 225 – A Roman judge named Ulpianus produced the first known mortality table for "annua," which were lifetime stipends made once per year in exchange for a lump-sum payment.

1600s

1600s – "Tontines" became popular with European governments to pay for wars and public works projects. A tontine gave each participant income for life, with the payments increasing to the survivors as other participants passed away. Payments ceased upon the death of all the participants.

1700s

1700s – British Parliament authorized annuity sales. Annuities became popular among European "high society," as a form of prevention of a fall from grace, unavailable in other, more risky investments.

1776

1776 – The National Pension Program for Soldiers was passed in America prior to the signing of the Declaration of Independence. It provided an annuity payment to soldiers and their families.

1812

1812 – The Pennsylvania Company for Granting Annuities was founded.

1905

1905 – Andrew Carnegie established the Teacher's Pension Fund in 1905. This eventually became TIAA—Teachers Insurance and Annuity Association—in 1918 to provide annuities to educators.

1930s

1930s – During the Great Depression, investors looked to annuities and life insurance as safe havens from financial ruin.

1935

1935 – President Franklin D. Roosevelt signed the Social Security Act. Social Security is essentially a lifetime income annuity.

1940

1940 – Ida May Fuller became first Social Security recipient. She receives 35 years' worth of payments for a total of $22,000.

1952

1952 – TIAA-CREF offered first variable deferred annuity, which enabled educators to invest part of their retirement in equities as a hedge against inflation.

1986

1986 – Congress passed tax reform that made deferred annuities one of the few financial products where you can invest unlimited amounts and get the benefit of tax deferral.

2010

2010 – Individual annuity sales in U.S. top $221 billion. (Source: LIMRA)

Annuities: Insure Your Investments

 Key Points from Chapter 5

1. Annuities are simply a RISK MANAGEMENT TOOL.

2. Annuities are not bad but there ARE "bad" annuities.

3. There are only two types of annuities – immediate or deferred.

4. Immediate annuities provide guaranteed income.

5. Deferred annuities provide tax-deferred growth with additional benefits and guarantees. There are two types of deferred annuities – fixed and variable.

6. Variable annuities offer many features and benefits that can literally allow you to "insure" your investments and have some peace of mind in turbulent times.

7. When it comes to market risk – manage it, put a floor under it, or eliminate it!

Chapter 6

Life Insurance: The Miracle Money Machine

In past chapters, I have discussed how changing trends in the economy, public policy, and overall life expectancy have completely altered the rules of the retirement game. By this point, though, I hope I have convinced you that there are real ways that you can still have the retirement of your dreams. In fact, I bet one of the reasons you are still reading this book is that I have promised to prove to you that you can have a guaranteed stream of income for the rest of your life – something you have just learned about with annuities.

But in today's changed world, what other options do you have to ensure that your family is provided for, your money is safe, your portfolio is optimized, and your money flow does not screech to a halt when your career finally does? How can you not only plan successfully for unforeseen expenses, but also for the ultimate foreseen expense? Here, life insurance makes its grand entrance. This chapter is all about how and why you should greet it with open arms and make it feel welcome in your retirement plan.

The Great Comeback

While it might strike you as morbid at first, planning your retirement with the inevitable in mind can enable you to retire more securely, eliminate anxiety about providing for your family, and give you rewarding cash returns in the long run. Having a plan for the long-term must be taken very seriously, and no retirement is complete without one. But having a plan in the form of some money put away in the bank for a retirement home is just not good enough. I see your plan and raise you cash value, tax benefits, estate and tax-free income creation, and the priceless feeling of knowing your family will be financially secure after you are gone.

Your grandparents relied on it to carry them through the Great Depression, as the life insurance industry prevailed without the serious problems experienced in other sectors of the economy. However, for most of you, the idea of life insurance might seem surprising – especially the concept of permanent life insurance. For the past 20 years, term life insurance has lit up the radar screen, while permanent life insurance has faded into the background. Why? The '80s and '90s saw a thriving stock market, more guaranteed pensions, and bigger Social Security checks, which made investing in a life insurance policy seem weak and ultra-risk-averse at a time when investing in the market promised to yield huge earnings – and in many cases, it did.

But today, with the stock market as unstable as it is, pensions disappearing like the dinosaurs, and Social Security in the throes of upheaval, that old permanent life policy that people scoffed at for years suddenly looks like the better deal for those headed into retirement. And that's because it is.

Some high-profile financial commentators have advised millions to skip permanent life insurance policies. Their advice was to "buy term and invest the difference." Unfortunately, an entire generation bought into that opinion. But rather than buying term and investing the difference, they bought term and spent the difference. Or, even worse, bought term and lost the difference! Now an entire generation of Americans is approaching retirement without any permanent life insurance. Where are these experts now who told people that their house would be paid off (it isn't), that they would have a pension (they don't), their kids would be on their own (they're not), and there would be no need for any life insurance (but there is)?

The Miracle of Life Insurance

The late Ben Feldman, one of the greatest life insurance salesman in history, often referred to life insurance as a miracle. Make no mistake about it: life insurance truly is a miracle in that it delivers exactly the right amount of money at exactly the right time. Think about it. What other financial instrument can guarantee a specific amount of dollars exactly when it is needed?

Feldman referred to life insurance as simply a drop of ink, a piece of paper, and a promise. Life insurance promises to:

Take care of your family if you die too soon.

They can live in the same home, attend the same schools, go to college, and maintain the lifestyle they are accustomed to even though you are not there to take care of them.

Take care of you if you live too long – the cash value of the policy can be withdrawn tax-free or turned into a lifetime income annuity.

Function as a self-completing plan. Even if you are disabled, a waiver of premiums can guarantee that your plan will be completed even if you are unable to make further premiums.

Provide immediate cash in the case of a terminal illness. Clients have used this cash to receive extraordinary medical treatment, which can delay death for many years. Others use it to get their affairs in order prior to death.

Provide long-term care benefits. Some policies now offer additional long-term care benefits in conjunction with the death benefit.

Feldman had a way of simplifying the concepts surrounding life insurance. Here are some of my favorite Feldman quotes on this subject:

"Life insurance is time. The time that man might not have. If he needs time, he needs life insurance."

"The basic purpose of life insurance is to create cash...nothing more and nothing less. Everything else confuses and complicates."

"Life insurance is the only tool that takes pennies and guarantees dollars."

Let me give you a perspective on life insurance that you may never have considered. Remember when I discussed the importance of mortality credits when using a lifetime income annuity in retirement? Life insurance uses those same mortality credits! How else could a 20-year-old write a check for $25 to an insurance company, leave the appointment, step in front of a speeding bus, and then have the family receive a check for $1 million from that insurance company? See, the insurance company knows that not many 20-year-olds are going to die, so a young person can take advantage of mortality credits through the miracle of life insurance. Some people call this leverage – and it is – but it is a very specific form of leverage that is based in mortality credits. Those same mortality credits allow an 85-year-old widow to write the insurance company a small check and receive large monthly payments for the rest of her life. Here is the deal: the risk to an insurance company when they write a life insurance policy is that the client will die too soon, while the risk when they write a lifetime income annuity is that the client will live too long. Because they are on both sides of longevity risk, the company can neutralize or even eliminate longevity risk. In doing so, they can provide you with the benefits you need and would not be able to have on your own.

Know Your Options

Although it may seem that I am steering you away from term insurance and favoring the permanent life insurance alternative (which, again, is not my opinion, but a conclusion based on cold, hard facts that I will share with you below), it is imperative that you know what your options are. Remember, doing your due diligence is an essential part of structuring a successful retirement plan. Term and permanent life insurance are both products based on your life expectancy, and they each come with entirely different benefits, policies, upsides, and downsides. Here is a rundown of what you should know about each.

Term Life Insurance

Choosing term life insurance is like renting a house. Instead of buying it outright, or making payments on it until it is yours for good, you pay a monthly rent to ensure you will have a home for the time you need one. Likewise, with term insurance, you make premium payments for a fixed amount of coverage (your death benefit) within a specific period of time. If you die during that period – usually between one and twenty years, depending on your age – your family gets to collect your death benefit. If you die after your term coverage has ended, they do not.

Term insurance is, essentially, rented insurance: it does not cover you for your entire life, but you are guaranteed coverage for a specific period of time, as long as you pay your premiums. One of the upsides of term insurance is that you can avoid paying large lump sums and instead pay smaller premiums on a monthly or quarterly basis. Conversely, you must continue to buy new term insurance policies as your coverage runs out at the end of each period – and premiums for term policies rise with your age. The premiums increase slowly at first but then rise quickly when you are above age 60 to the point where you will have to drop it because the premiums are just too high.

Here's why: life insurance is a product based on your life expectancy. As you get older, your life expectancy changes, and so must your term life insurance policy. There are several types of term insurance. Increasing premium term is the basic term policy, and it will be the cheapest term available. Under this policy, the term premium goes up each year. There are also 5-year, 10-year, 20-year, and even 30-year term policies. With these policies, you will pay the same premium for the entire term. In effect, you will overpay for the first half of the term and underpay for the rest of the term (in comparison to the increasing premium term). While these policies may seem like a good deal and a logical alternative to the increasing term policy, they are almost a guaranteed money-loser once you consider the lapse rates of term products. The lapse rate is the number of term policies cancelled prior to expiration. With lapse rates well over 50% at 10 years, all of those people paid more than they should have. If you really believe in level premium term, why not level the premium to age 100 or age 121? That is, after all, precisely what a permanent life policy can offer (see next section).

An offshoot term policy is called term with premium re-fund. I like the sizzle that this policy offers: you pay a set premium for 20 years. If you die, it pays the death benefit. If you live, at the end of the 20 years you get all of your money back!

When you take this policy apart, it is actually a permanent policy that has been set up to refund your premiums. Again, you are overpaying in the early years to underpay later on. It just has a nice bonus to it in the refund feature that many people find attractive. Nevertheless, the only policy that matters is the one that is in force on the day you die (but any policy is still better than no policy).

A type of term insurance that is disappearing is called decreasing term. In the past, these were used with a mortgage or other type of loan and were structured so the amount of life insurance would go down as the loan principal went down. I think it is disappearing because term insurance is already so inexpensive that it does not make sense for the death benefit to decrease each year. When you add the facts that most people are significantly underinsured anyway and that the administrative costs of these policies can be quite high, it is no wonder that these policies have pretty much disappeared from the scene.

 Sample Insurance Premiums By the Numbers

10-Year Guaranteed Level Term Life Insurance Sample Monthly Premiums:

	Women		Men	
Age	$250,000	$500,000	$250,000	$500,000
30	$14	$21	$14	$22
35	$14	$22	$15	$23
40	$16	$26	$17	$29
45	$19	$31	$20	$34
50	$26	$45	$29	$53

Sample Monthly Premiums:

Issue Age	Women		Men	
	$10,000	$50,000	$10,000	$50,000
45-49	$8.93	$28.67	$11.42	$41.08
50-54	$10.46	$36.29	$13.41	$51.04
55-59	$14.38	$55.92	$18.12	$74.58
60-64	$20.44	$86.21	$24.85	$108.25
65-69	$27.38	$120.88	$31.99	$143.96
70-74	$39.83	$183.13	$44.65	$207.25

Source: AARP Level Benefit Term Life Insurance from New York Life, http://www.nylaarp.com/
Life-Insurance/Level-Benefit-Term.
Sample rates, actual rates will vary. Premiums increase as insured enters each new age range.

Many people, especially in the past few decades, have claimed just this sort of common sense when explaining their decisions to opt for term life insurance. Why pay more money for unending coverage when all you want is to ensure that your life insurance holds up until your children are self-sufficient? This mindset might have been sharp 20 years ago, but today it faces a harsh reality check as the age at which a young adult's self-sufficiency kicks in continues to rise dramatically.

Your retirement money is yours – not your children's. You have done more for them than they probably know, and retirement is a time to focus on yourself. Still, more than half of today's young people (the Gen-Y'ers who make up the largest chunk of the U.S. population since baby boomers) move back home after graduating from college. In 2007, a *Newsweek* article on the embattled future of retirement cited research that showed senior citizens in over 21 countries were giving more money to their kids than they received each year. And this same article told of something even more relevant to your own retirement plan: in America, 28% of 22- to 29-year-olds depend on money from their parents to cover "major expenses." Here is my advice: let life insurance handle your legacy to your children so you do not have to sacrifice your own happiness and retirement pleasure to help your kids out while you are alive. If your children are guaranteed money in the form of a death benefit in the future, their immediate and financial planning needs will be alleviated and you will be able to exercise your right to use your money the way you have always wanted to.

That said, even if you are going to take the term insurance route and plan to cancel when your children do not need monetary support anymore, you are looking at a long duration of premiums and term renewals. In addition, the chances that you will die while covered by your term insurance are spectacularly low. Think about this: only about 1% of people with term life insurance policies actually die within their term of coverage. That means that 99% of people with term policies die outside of their period of coverage, leaving their spouses and children behind with no death benefit at all.

Still, choosing the term insurance path then dropping coverage at around age 60 remains a popular course of action, although it is losing ground. Consider the story of Paul and Stacey Brush. Both are 35, and they have a 2-year-old son, Dylan. The Brushes envision their only child striding across the stage and receiving his diploma from the dean of a well-respected, four-year private college – 20 years from now. Estimating their future expenses with inflation in mind, they decide they need to provide at least $250,000 for his college costs in case something happens to them. They take out a 20-year term life insurance policy with a $300,000 death benefit for the cost of $250 a year. Paul and Stacey can rest easy knowing Dylan will have enough money to pay for college no matter what happens to them in the next two decades.

The problem with the logic of this scenario – which, no doubt, is reality for many people – is that now, more than ever, life insurance is not just about paying for college or ensuring the well-being of your family if you die prematurely. A June 2011 article in *Kiplinger's* magazine heralded a new era of "common sense" when it comes to life insurance and retirement, noting that "with the mortgage paid, the kids on their own, and Medicare and Social Security on the way, common sense suggested you could safely let your insurance expire" in the past, but not so anymore. Life insurance needs are no longer temporary, like funding Dylan's college education or paying off the mortgage. Your life insurance needs are permanent. Longer life expectancies, no pensions, and greater expenses eating into personal assets have created a retirement revolution. And leading you safely out of the frenzied upheaval is the permanent life solution.

Permanent Life Insurance

With permanent life insurance, you do not rent the home – you buy it. No one can take it away; it is yours for the long haul. The kind of life insurance you own for life.

The price is heftier than it is for term insurance, but a permanent life policy can be bought at an optimal rate if you pay a lump sum. Other options include a series of premium payments over the course of a few years until you pay off the full amount. Because of average life expectancies, permanent life insurance costs increase the older you are when you purchase it.

There are several types of permanent life insurance. Whole life is the oldest variation and has proven to be a bellwether policy in good times and bad. Although less popular today, it is not because of poor performance. In fact, it has done just the opposite. If you were to ask a handful of wealthy people what the best investment they have made over the past 15 or 20 years has been, many would say their whole life policy. Typically, mutual insurance companies sell these policies, and mutual companies are owned by their policy owners. As such, they pay dividends not to stockholders (since there are none), but to the holders of "participating policies." Whole life is a participating policy. The reason whole life sales have decreased is that the number of mutual companies has been drastically reduced. In the roaring '90s, many of the traditional mutual companies like MetLife, Prudential, John Hancock, and countless others demutualized and became stock companies. As a stock company, they have to pay dividends to stockholders. Stockholders do not want large sums of money paid to policyholders, so whole life appears much less attractive to them. There are a number of other reasons why whole life sales have decreased, mostly dealing with profit margins, reserve requirements, and other such complications. The main reason, though, is that there are only a handful of mutual companies remaining – New York Life, Northwestern Mutual, Guardian, State Farm Life, Mass Mutual, Mutual of Omaha, and a few others.

Regardless, market trends should not deter you from purchasing a whole life policy. Whole life is actually quite an attractive form of life insurance because it has a guaranteed premium. This means premiums will never go up. Whole life also offers a guaranteed death benefit and a guaranteed cash value, so you know exactly what you are getting before you buy. In addition, the policy pays dividends each year. While most companies have paid dividends every year in the past, they are not guaranteed. Dividends can also go up or down depending on company performance and economic conditions.

It is true that you could technically save money on premium costs by buying term insurance policies in your younger years. However, your premiums would rise dramatically as you got older. Whole life premiums, by contrast, cost a little more up front but do not increase in later years. Here is what I mean:

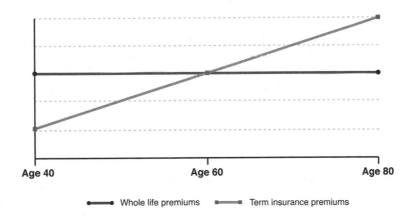

Age 40   Age 60   Age 80

●━━━● Whole life premiums   ■━━━■ Term insurance premiums

It might seem like a simple trade-off – shelling out more money for more death benefit security. However, whole life insurance has other benefits up its sleeve to make you see the light. First off, let's revisit the fact that as soon as you fully pay your whole life premium (many policies offer paid up options after so many years), you are guaranteed life insurance coverage for your entire life, and your family is guaranteed a death benefit no matter when you die. Let me say that magic word one more time: guaranteed. Sounds good, right? It's about to sound even better. Whole life insurance isn't just a forever-brand of term life insurance. It is a whole different animal; and, like I said, one that has a lot more benefits.

The two main parts of whole life insurance are the death benefit and the cash value. Obviously, the death benefit is what people expect from a life insurance policy, but what makes it special is that it is guaranteed for life. Essentially, for a fixed premium – that will not rise with your age if you decide to pay it off over a number of years – you are buying irrevocable and bulletproof security for your family once you are gone. But the biggest twist is this: whole life insurance does not just stash away money for your spouse and children to use when you are gone; it also builds up extra money for you to use while you are still here. This living benefit component is called cash value, and it will be an essential part of your retirement plan. This chart might make the two-part plan a bit clearer:

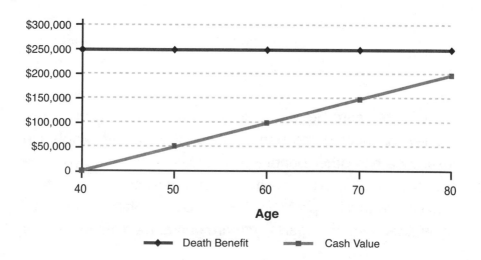

The cash value in a whole life policy is composed of two parts: a guaranteed cash value and compounded dividends. The guaranteed cash value starts very low but increases every year – regardless of market conditions or interest rates. The dividends that the policy earns also go into the cash value. As an extra bonus, these dividends also purchase additional paid-up insurance. On top of that, each year those dividends also earn dividends. So your cash value goes up every year and your death benefit rises as well. Your policy will say that dividends are not guaranteed, and they are not. However, most companies have many decades of track records for paying dividends. More likely, if you buy a policy like this in a high interest rate environment, as interest rates fall, your dividend rate may not keep up with your initial projection. The company will still pay dividends, just not as high as you may have hoped. Conversely, if you buy one of these policies in a low interest rate environment, you may actually see your dividends increase over time – exceeding your expectations.

You need to note that whole life policies typically have high surrender charges in the early years. Surrender charges are fees that are assessed if you withdraw money from the cash value. These charges phase out over time. If you have made the purchase for the long term and the premium fits your budget, these charges should not alarm you. The cash value growth is tax-deferred, similar to a 401(k) or traditional IRA. The cash value can be borrowed at very low interest rates for whatever you please – emergencies, the mortgage, college tuition, or that dream vacation. In fact, if you have ever heard the radio commercial "bank on yourself," they are talking about the loan and withdrawal provisions of permanent life insurance.

Back in the 1980s, another form of permanent insurance called universal life became all the rage. If you remember, interest rates paid by banks and money market funds were very high during this time. Whole life dividends seemed less and less attractive until universal life was born. (I remember when some of these policies were paying 13% and 14% interest!) A universal life policy is really a permanent policy that combines a term life insurance policy with a tax-deferred, guaranteed interest fixed savings account. A portion of the premium covers the cost of insurance and any of the policy's fees. The rest of the premium goes into the savings account and earns interest. These interest rates then go up or down based on market rates. The cash value grows tax-deferred and you can take out loans or withdrawals, generally tax-free (loans are almost always tax-free; withdrawals are tax-free up to the basis in the contract – typically the total of your premiums). You maintain control of your premiums. You can raise your premiums to save more, lower your premiums within the guidelines of the contract, and even stop your premiums as long as there is enough cash value to keep your monthly life insurance and administrative costs covered.

You can raise your life insurance death benefit (subject to company approval) or lower your coverage if you decide you have too much – the policy is extremely flexible. I have seen firsthand how powerful this flexibility can be. If someone loses a job, they can stop paying premiums for a while and then restart once they are back to work. I have seen businesses saved by the loan provision of the policy. However, I have also seen that flexibility allow people to hurt themselves. Because they could lower the premium, they did. But as they aged, that monthly cost of insurance rose as well (remember, it is part term life insurance). It eventually got to the point where they could no longer afford the policy and had to let it go. Universal life premiums are typically lower than whole life premiums, but the policy will perform better the more money you put into it.

The next type of permanent insurance is variable life insurance. It comes in two flavors – variable whole life and variable universal life. Variable whole life is almost non-existent in the industry today. Variable universal life is the most common. In fact, it is the type of policy of which I own the most. I do own whole life and term as well but there is a special place in my heart for variable universal life. One of the reasons for this is that I was the National VUL Sales Manager for a Fortune 100 life insurance company back in the early '90s. Through this experience, I got to know the policy inside and out. And it was quite a catch in the 1990s – the stock market was going up 20%-30% nearly every year. Universal life rates had come down to the 7% range. Whole life was considered boring. So along came variable universal life. This product works in the same way universal life does, with one big exception – instead of putting your money into a fixed savings account, you could now diversify across numerous investment divisions – which are essentially variable investment options within the policy. With VUL you now had the unlimited upside of the market, tax-deferred growth, tax-free withdrawals (up to basis – amount of your premiums), and tax-free loans! It really is an incredible product for any bull market.

However, as we know, markets do not just go up. Just as you have the unlimited upside of the market, you also have the unlimited downside. So how can I still like variable universal life? Simple. The people who like this product are the people who do not buy whole life or universal life because they think they can do better. I am one of those people. While I do not try to time the market, I make a few moves each year and I have done extremely well through good times and bad. Over the long run, the stock market should persevere. The policies now allow me to invest in commodities and emerging markets too through the underlying variable investment options. This policy is a wonderful alternative for the people who want to buy term and invest the difference. See, if you buy term insurance on your own, that money is gone. However, all premiums made (including those for the term costs) to the universal life policies count toward the cost basis of the policy. Without getting too far into detail, you effectively are receiving tax advantaged term life insurance.

There are drawbacks of course, in addition to exposure to stock market risk, variable life insurance policies carry mortality and expense charges, insurance charges, administrative charges, and possible surrender charges. However, when you compare these fees to the tax advantages gained over the life of these policies, it may make sense for some folks. The only policy that matters is the one that is in force on the day you die. You have to buy the policy that works for you.

A more recent offering in the universal life arena is indexed life. The concept here is similar. It is a universal life policy in which your money goes into an indexed savings account as opposed to a fixed savings account. This index can be one of any of a number of indices – the most common being the S&P 500 index. Here, the amount of interest you receive is based on a fairly complicated formula derived from the performance of the index. These policies, again, imply that you get some of the upside potential of the market without any of the downside. I have seen some very interesting products recently show up in this Indexed Life space. One Minneapolis based insurer has a very simple policy – the downside floor is 0, the upside cap is currently 11%. If the market went up 9%, your policy would be credited with 9%. If the market went up 23%, your policy would be credited with 11%. If the market went down 23%, your policy would be credited with 0%. Remember, these caps and floors can change so read the fine print to see what is contractually guaranteed. These policies have actually performed decently over the last decade because they do not go down with down markets. Here is the conclusion: in down markets, these products can do fine, but in bull markets, clients may be disappointed by the reduced upside they really get to experience. It is really up to what the client is looking for and the trade-off of upside potential vs. downside protection. If you are considering indexed life insurance, you will also want to ask questions about liquidity, flexibility, and surrender charges.

The Investment of a Lifetime

The prospect of being able to preserve wealth within an industry that is as relatively safe as the life insurance industry can be somewhat of a beacon of hope for people struggling to preserve their money in an increasingly volatile market. The cash value component of whole life insurance is essentially a steady, long-term benefit simply by merit of its dependability and security as it is guaranteed – two things that are hard to come by in the current economic climate.

Think of life insurance cash value as your financial bunker that can provide you with safety during difficult financial times. It is not meant to be a speedy, risky investment for you to gamble with. In fact, a whole life insurance policy gives you just the opposite: your cash value offers the certain and stable returns you need in order to take more risks with your other investments. Your whole life cash value will actually help to optimize your portfolio, as you will have more flexibility to invest and spend while maintaining your lifestyle and still leaving a legacy to your loved ones – a benefit not possible under the constraints of term life insurance.

In an era of instant gratification and fast turnaround, the living benefit of whole life insurance is often overlooked in favor of riskier investments with quicker returns. A whole life policy may take more time to show its value, but your cash value can exceed the premiums you paid in around 8 to 10 years. In the long-term, whole life cash value can provide a source of funds for emergency or other needs – all it requires is a little patience.

Tax Benefits

As if these living benefits were not enough, your whole life insurance policy can also offer a slew of tax benefits. Instead of withdrawing money from your policy, you can borrow against your life insurance cash value for a source of instant credit. In less time than it would take you to merely apply for a loan from the bank, you can call your insurance company, request a check or wire transfer, and have your money right away.

The cash that you are borrowing has been accumulating tax-deferred, which means that, just like a traditional IRA or 401(k), there is no tax due until you withdraw the money. In fact, you can withdraw up to the total amount of premiums paid, or borrow any amount, tax-free – your insurance company will not ask you any questions, or check your credit, either. As long as you pay back your loans when you can, your death benefit remains untouched.

This great advantage even extends past you and reaches your family and future grandchildren – there is no income tax on your death benefit, either. If structured properly, your family can also avoid estate tax on your death benefit, allowing you to vastly increase the size of the estate you leave behind. By putting your life insurance policy in an irrevocable trust at least three years before your death, you can make sure that your family will save big on estate taxes. Since the life insurance is no longer your personal asset once it's in the trust, it is no longer considered part of your estate. Your trust fund is like your own bulletproof vault, protecting what belongs to your family from depletion by taxation.

 ## How much life insurance should I have? – By the Numbers

The recent economic turmoil and weak job market are rough on savings and retirement planning. They also complicate the issue of how much life insurance is right for you and your family, and what kind you should buy. The answer is not really how much life insurance *you* need – it is how much money your family will need after you are gone. Ask yourself:

- How much money will my family need after my death to meet immediate expenses, like funeral expenses and debts?

- How much money will my family need to maintain their standard of living over the long term?

Life insurance proceeds can help pay immediate expenses, including uncovered medical costs, funeral expenses, final estate settlement costs, taxes, and other lump-sum obligations such as outstanding debts and mortgage balances. They can also help your family cover future financial obligations like everyday living expenses, college, your spouse's retirement, and so much more.

When people sit down and figure out how much their family would really need, they are often shocked at the amount. Even families of modest incomes can have life insurance needs in the millions. Yet many only have $100,000 or $250,000 of group supplemental term life insurance from their employer. There are several ways to calculate how much is enough.

Income Replacement

Simply calculate how much money it would

take to replace your income. For example, if you earn $50,000 per year, it would take $1,000,000 earning 5% to provide that. However, at the current 1% that CDs are paying, it would take $5,000,000! And that is before we figure out future pay increases or inflation. In this low interest rate environment, you can see how easy it is to be underinsured.

Human Life Value

You will literally earn a fortune over your lifetime. If you had a machine in your garage that produced your income each year along with regular promotions and pay raises, what would it be worth? Millions of dollars! You would certainly insure that machine. Well, that machine is you. What is the present value of all of your future earnings? That is the amount that should be covered under this formula.

Financial Needs Approach

This is really a simple strategy to calculate how much coverage to buy and to form a plan that is easy to update. The idea is to assess whether you need extra coverage or different policies only after you project your life insurance needs as the sum of four categories.

- **Final Expenses**. A funeral, burial, and related expenses tend to cost $10,000 to $20,000. Put the number that you feel is appropriate for your family.

- **Mortgages and Other Debts**. Add up your mortgage balance, car loans, student loans, and any other debts that would be a burden on your survivors. They may choose not to pay off the mortgage, especially if the interest rate is low, but the money should be available so that they won't have to sell or move.

- **College Expenses**. This calculation can be challenging because you need to consider the cost of college at the time your kids enroll. Your spouse may also want to get some further education. Decide whether you want the insurance to cover all or a portion of the tab, then add the amount to your life insurance calculation.

- **Income Replacement**. Once you cover funeral expenses, debts, and education, your family may not need to replace 100% of your income. So decide how much income your family would need and what interest rate should be used.

Add all four categories to estimate how much life insurance is appropriate, then adjust the number to reflect any special circumstances. You might increase it if you do not have a pension, but you could decrease your coverage if your spouse earns a substantial salary. If you or a family member has a significant medical history, add more. If you are the one with the medical condition, you will find it tough to buy additional coverage later at a price you can afford.

No matter which formula you use, you will see that you need more than you probably thought. It is acceptable to use term insurance for some of these needs. Term is very inexpensive over the short term. You should have some permanent life insurance as well.

It may seem like life insurance could be a do-it-yourself project, but I believe there is no substitute for the guidance and assistance you will get by meeting with a qualified insurance agent or other financial professional. So if you are serious about protecting your family's future, contact an insurance professional in your community.

Tax Diversification

We all know the importance of asset allocation and diversification of investments. When we think of diversification,
we normally think of spreading our money among stocks,
bonds, commodities, cash, etc. Don't put all of your eggs
in one basket. By diversifying your assets, you typically
smooth out the ups and downs since, historically, not all
asset classes move up or down together. (More recently,
we have had times when all of these assets have gone up
or down together, so the search for assets that are non-
correlated continues to be a very important part of diversification.)

But what about tax diversification? This is a very important concept to understand. If you think about it, most
people have the majority of their assets in qualified or pre-
tax accounts such as 401(k)s, TSAs and IRAs. These vehicles offer tremendous tax advantages in the accumulation phase. The contributions are tax deductible and offer
tax-deferred growth. However, in the distribution phase,
they can be a tax nightmare since all distributions are
fully taxable. With all of the economic problems facing this
country, where do you think tax rates are going? I can tell
you the math is very clear – taxes will be going up, I have
no doubt about that. If you agree with that proposition, my
question is this: how much sense does it make to have all
or most of your money in fully taxable accounts? Would
it have been better to have some of that money invested
where withdrawals would be tax-free?

If you could invest in the "tax perfect" retirement plan,
what would it look like? It would probably include:

1. Contributions that are **tax deductible.**

2. Accumulation that is **tax deferred.**

3. Distributions that are **tax-free.**

Unfortunately, such a plan does not exist. But you may be able to get either 1 and 2 or 2 and 3. Many people increasingly like the idea of paying taxes now on savings for retirement, knowing that they will not have to pay taxes on the growth *or* the distribution of that savings! The most common financial vehicles that do that are a Roth IRA, tax-free municipal bonds, and cash value life insurance. I like to say it this way: if you were a farmer, would you rather pay tax on the seed or the harvest? I think almost every farmer would rather pay tax on the seed. It works the same way with money.

I am a big supporter of Roth IRAs. But Roth IRAs do not allow unlimited contributions. Tax-free bonds can work, but you need to be very careful since many states and municipalities are having significant financial issues. Additionally, as interest rates rise, the value of the bonds will go down.

Permanent life insurance that builds cash value can be a great tool in this situation. The premiums are paid with after-tax dollars. The policy's cash value grows tax-deferred and you can access cash values before or after retirement on a tax-free basis as long as it is structured properly! Upon death, the death benefit is paid to your beneficiaries tax-free.

Just take a look at this example of taking $100,000 in income – all from a pension plan, such as a 401(k) or IRA. Under today's tax brackets, if there were no additional income, that would put this person in a 25% tax bracket resulting in a

$25,000 tax (assuming no deductions for the sake of simplicity) – leaving $75,000 to spend after taxes.

Retirement Income of $100,000		
Without Tax Diversification	**Tax Diversification Strategy**	
$100,000	$50,000	$50,000[3]
401(k) / Qualified Plans	401(k) / Qualified Plans	Cash Value Life Insurance
100% taxable	100% taxable	tax free[2]
$100,000 taxed at 25%[1]	$50,000 taxed at 15%[1]	$50,000 taxed at 0%[2]
= $25,000 tax	= $7,500 tax	= $0 tax
$75,000 to spend after taxes	**$92,500 to spend after taxes**	

Hypothetical example for illustrative purposes only   Source: New York Life Insurance Company
[1] Assumed marginal federal income tax bracket under current rates for married filing jointly.
[2] If structured properly. Policy loans and partial policy value surrenders will reduce the death benefit of the policy and may cause the life insurance policy to lapse. Distributions exceeding cost basis will result in taxation.
[3] The cash value in a life insurance policy is accessed through policy loans, which accrue interest at the current rate, and cash withdrawals and loans will decrease the total death benefit and total cash value. Policy values are based on non-guaranteed factors, such as dividends and interest rates, which are subject to change. Therefore, the supplemental retirement income is not guaranteed.

However, if for instance, we took $50,000 from a totally taxable qualified pension plan and $50,000 from a tax-free bucket of money, there would be no tax on part – and a lowered bracket and tax on the half we do have to pay taxes on – leaving over $92,000 to spend! It's clear that in this example, by employing a tax diversification strategy and moving a portion of your money into a cash value life insurance policy, you can potentially lower your taxes while giving you more to spend – to increase your standard of living!

Legacy Planning

Speaking of your family, let's talk a little bit about what everyone secretly wants to know: after you are gone, what will your family legacy be? While a life insurance policy certainly cannot determine what your entire legacy will be, it can take care of the monetary part for you (let's hope you have got the other stuff covered). Using your cash value as an estate planning tool is one of the smartest and safest ways to add to your estate – or even create one out of thin air.

Consider the case of Joanne, a 65-year-old grandmother who wants to make sure that each of her children – and grandchildren – receive a nice sum of money upon her death. Her estate is to be divided up among her five grown children, but Joanne needs to decide how to provide legacy gifts for her six grandchildren. Outside of her retirement funds, all Joanne has is a $100,000 Certificate of Deposit, which she had originally planned to use to fund her grandchildrens' share of money upon her death. Here's the problem: that $100,000 CD will essentially remain a $100,000 CD until the day she dies, only accumulating additional value based on a meager rate of 1% annually (today's rates) for a final amount of around $110,500 in ten years. (And don't forget taxes!)

If Joanne goes this route, each of her grandchildren will receive about $18,400 upon her death if she passes away at 75. That is all well and good, but what Joanne really wants is to increase the amount of wealth she has to distribute to her grandkids so she can ensure they all get a substantial gift when she is gone. Enter life insurance – to the rescue, once again.

By taking out a single premium universal life insurance policy and naming her grandchildren as the beneficiaries, Joanne is able to purchase a policy with a death benefit more than double the amount of her premium – making her new legacy gift instantly twice the size! Let's say this policy Joanne buys for $100,000 has a $220,000 guaranteed death benefit. Now, instead of $18,400, each of her grandkids is guaranteed $36,667 – and it can all be passed along to them income tax-free. As if that is not enough, Joanne also retains the benefit to access all of the cash value of the policy during her lifetime in case of an emergency or any unforeseen expenses.

Some other ways that retirees use life insurance include the following:

- Using life insurance to leverage charitable giving. If a couple was planning on giving $50,000 to a charity, by using life insurance they could put the $50,000 into a life insurance policy that would pay the charity $100,000 or more upon death. If they use a policy with a money back guarantee, they still have access to those funds in case of an emergency.

- Using life insurance to cover final expenses. John and Leslie, both age 70, had saved $10,000 each for their final expenses. They didn't want to be a burden on their family. However, that $10,000 buys less and less each year. Yet they have no more money to put into their final expenses savings account. Their financial advisor recommends they each put their $10,000 into a single premium universal life policy. This policy was guaranteed not to lapse and had a money-back guarantee at any time – so their money remained liquid in case of an emergency. They now have $32,000 of final expense coverage ($15,000 on John and $17,000 on Leslie) that will be available when they die.

- Using life insurance to cover the loss of Social Security or pension upon death. There is even a strategy called "pension maximization" where a person would select a single life payout on their pension (instead of joint life with their spouse) and use the higher pension amount (than it would have been for a joint life payout) to purchase a life insurance policy. The advantages are that if the non-pension spouse happened to die first, the higher pension check would still come for the rest of the pensioner's life. Additionally, putting the extra money in a whole life insurance policy could build cash value for an additional check in the future. One drawback of this approach is that the higher pension amount might not purchase enough life insurance to protect the other spouse if the pension collecting spouse were to die. I recommend getting help from a financial advisor if you are considering this strategy.

The Longevity Gap: Avoiding Crisis for Women

As you wade into the sometimes-murky waters of choosing life insurance coverage, keep in mind that just as retirement has changed in recent years, so, in a way, has life insurance. While life insurance itself is the same old friend that has helped millions of Americans safely ride out numerous depressions and recessions, take out loans to launch businesses, and provide for their widows, it means something different to retirees today than it has in the past.

Put simply, retirement is not what it used to be, and you will need more income over a longer period of time than your parents did. That said, you will also have a much longer retirement than your parents did. Americans used to start working early in life, retire late, and die early. Now, they start working later in life, retire earlier, and die later. You know how I love facts; how's this for one? While your grandparents saw between 5 and 10 years of retirement on average, your generation is looking at closer to 30.

I want to stress the significance of longer life expectancy, and what it means for you and yours. Now more than ever, retirees have to rely on their personal savings and assets to ensure they can pay for basic living expenses after retiring. This fact, coupled with the startling statistics that women live an average of 5.2 years longer than men and 7 out of 10 baby boomer women will become widows – and afterwards live for another 15-25 years – signals a looming crisis that only life insurance can ultimately resolve. If you are married, remember that there is a 50/50 chance that either you or your spouse will live to be 92 years old.

Even though women generally live longer than men, they come up short when it comes to planning ahead for their futures. When deciding on life insurance, couples need to understand the pressing need for husbands and wives to plan together for retirement, as wives will most likely be the ones reaping the consequences – and benefits – of whatever plan is chosen. A life insurance policy is the only option that guarantees to husbands that they will provide for their wives – or vice versa – when they pass away.

Essentially, when you think ahead about providing for a surviving spouse, you need to account for what income is going to die with you. If you are lucky enough to receive a pension in retirement, those checks may stop coming after you are gone. In addition, Social Security payments go down with the death of a spouse. The spouse you leave behind will have reduced sources of income; this can be a devastating financial blow without proper planning.

As I have discussed in this chapter, life insurance offers you solutions to a plethora of problems faced by baby boomers in the next few years. One of the biggest problems of them all is the predicament boomer women will face if they do not plan for retirement with the inevitable in mind, so that the death of a spouse does not leave them struggling and nearly broke. Life insurance is the best way to replace money that will be lost by having a reduced Social Security check, and it is the best way to guarantee that you and your spouse will keep making money for the rest of your lives.

Death is a permanent problem that we all have to face. It should be solved with permanent life insurance.

 For more information...

A great resource to learn more about life insurance is www.lifehappens.org. The CEO of this organization is Marv Feldman, another friend of mine. Marv is the son of the legendary Ben Feldman (whom I introduced to you at the beginning of this chapter). Marv was just awarded the

John Newton Russell Award. The *Russell* award is the highest honor accorded by the insurance industry to a living individual who has rendered outstanding services to the institution of life insurance. Mr. Feldman's father, Ben Feldman, was a past recipient of this prestigious award in 1984. This marks the first time in the 70-year history of the award that one family can claim two winners of the award. Ben's granddaughter, Wendy, is the former mayor of Queen Creek, AZ, and is my agent.

Life Insurance: The Miracle Money Machine

Key Points from Chapter 6

1. If you were to die, how much money would be needed to allow your family to continue as if you hadn't?

2. Term life insurance is like renting. Premiums are low initially but rise significantly over time. There is no cash value. Less than 1% of term policies ever pay a death a claim.

3. Permanent life insurance is like owning. Premiums are higher but build cash value that grows tax deferred and can be withdrawn or borrowed out tax-free.

4. Permanent life insurance comes in many flavors – whole life, universal life, variable life, and indexed life.

5. Since women live longer than men and typically marry older men, they can look forward to a widowhood of 10, 20, even 30 years. They will live with the consequences of how much life insurance is on the man in their life.

6. Understand the importance of *tax diversification*. Use Roth IRAs and permanent life to help tax diversify your retirement.

Chapter 7

Long-Term Care Insurance: What Is Your Plan?

No retirement plan is complete without a plan for long-term care. For many seniors, it is the only thing they have not planned for that could completely wipe out their entire life's work and savings. Think about that for a minute. If your house burned to the ground, it would be an emotional loss but your insurance would cover the move or rebuild. If you totaled your car, you may have some physical injuries, but the insurance company would protect you from lawsuits and replace your car. But what would happen if you needed full-time, around-the-clock care to help you live your life? What would that cost? How long would your savings last? What would happen to your spouse and family?

The Odds That You Will Need Long-Term Care Insurance

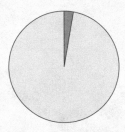

Odds of Having a Fire?
About 3%

Here are some interesting statistics: The odds of your home burning down between now and the day you die are about 3 out of 100 (3%), but nearly every homeowner has homeowner's insurance.

The odds of you totaling your car between now and the day you die are about 18 out of 100 (18%), yet nearly every automobile owner carries auto insurance.

Odds of a Car Accident?
About 18%

Odds of Needing Long-Term Care Insurance?
About 72%

The odds that you will need some form of long-term care between now and the day you die are about 72 out of 100 (72%). However, less than 30% of Americans over the age of 45 have purchased long-term care insurance.

Source: The 2010 Sourcebook for Long-Term Care Insurance, American Association for Long-Term Care Insurance, data by Milliman Consulting (2010).

What is Long-Term Care?

Long-term care is defined as the type of care given when someone needs assistance with the "Activities of Daily Living" (ADL) due to an illness, accident, or old age. This assistance can be given at home or in a facility. Long-term care is not one service, but many different services that provide people the help they need when a prolonged illness or disability keeps them from being able to care for themselves. It can range from help with day-to-day activities in the home to more sophisticated services such as skilled nursing care in your home, an assisted living facility, or a nursing facility.

 Activities of Daily Living (ADLs)

Bathing	Eating
Dressing	Using the toilet
Continence	Transferring (getting out of bed, chair, car, walking around, etc.)

Skilled care and custodial (or personal) care remain the most common terms used to describe long-term care and the level of assistance a person may need. Skilled care is generally needed for medical conditions that require care from a physician, registered nurse, professional therapist or other skilled medical personnel. Skilled care is usually provided 24 hours a day, is ordered by a doctor, includes some type of treatment plan and is generally provided in a nursing home. It can also be conducted in your home with visiting nurses and other professionals. Custodial helps a person with their activities of daily living. It is less involved than skilled care and can be performed at home, adult daycare centers, assisted living facilities, or nursing homes.

The Costs: Financial and Emotional

Long-term care can be very expensive, and not just in financial terms. It can literally tear families apart; it can ruin the health of the caregiver in the family; and, of course, it can wipe out savings. While nursing home and home healthcare service costs differ across the country, here are some common averages:

- The private pay rate for a nursing facility is $76,416 per year.*

- The private pay rate for a Medicare-certified home health agency is $25.86 per hour.*

*Source: New York Life Cost of Care Survey for Nursing Homes and Survey for Home Care Costs (2008)

Here is a hypothetical example. Let's say that mom needs long-term care assistance. For now, a few hours a day from family members or adult daycare is enough. As time goes by, mom needs full time care from a nursing home. Just from this example, look at the potential costs: a year of care four hours per day, followed by a year of eight hours per day, followed by three years in a nursing home. Using today's costs, the total would be nearly $300,000! That leads to a couple of questions. First, where is mom going to get that money? And second, what would your costs look like in 20 or 30 years when you might need the same type of care? The only way you will have the money for this type of expense is to plan well in advance.

When you first need long-term care, who do you think will provide care first? Of course it will be your family. They are right there; they love you and want to help you. But you have to realize the toll that providing this care will take on them. Being a caregiver is very expensive and can cause financial challenges. Your family will likely have to take time off from work and will spend their own money on all of the extras (e.g., medicine, walkers, canes, grab bars, etc.) that you need. They will have to pay someone to be with you when they cannot be there.

We have not even discussed the tremendous emotional challenges that caring for a loved one entails. Many people find themselves in the "sandwich generation" where they are not only caring for their children but their parents as well! This role reversal of children taking care of their parents is incredibly difficult emotionally. Balancing all of these priorities certainly increases both emotional and financial stress.

Providing care is a physical challenge for most care givers. Lifting someone into or out of a bed or a bath tub, moving from the living room to the kitchen, dressing someone, and feeding them all takes a toll. And remember, this is full time, 24/7 care. Caregivers can suffer hernias, back problems, or other physical issues.

Long-term care really is not about *you*, it is about your family! Since your family is on the front lines, consider what you can do to make their lives a little easier when it comes to giving care.

Who Pays for Long-Term Care?

Many people think their health insurance or Medicare or some government program will pay for their long-term care. The truth is that personal health insurance and government programs do not cover the majority of long-term care costs. Health insurance covers medical costs such as tests, medicines, doctor visits, hospitalization, or other specific services. It will not pay for long-term care costs.

Government programs are restricted or limited when it comes to paying for long-term care. Medicare, for example, provides health insurance for people over age 65 and pays only 5% of long-term care costs nationally. It covers acute care, such as you would receive from doctors in a hospital. Medicare pays for skilled care from medical professionals, but does not generally cover custodial care, which is another term for assistance with activities of daily living. Additionally, in order to qualify for whatever care Medicare will cover, you must have a three-day qualifying hospital stay – something that may not occur as you age naturally, and might not precede your need for help with tasks like bathing and dressing.

Medicare covers some home care under Part B, but the services must be "medically necessary" – a Medicare term that means "supplies or services that are needed for the diagnosis or treatment of your medical condition." (*Medicare & You*, p.37, 129; 2011) Medicare requires that home care services be ordered by a doctor and that you are receiving skilled treatment for an illness or injury. Help with bathing, dressing, and toileting are not considered medically necessary – they are considered custodial care, not acute care.

Remember, Medicare does not pay for room and board at an assisted living facility or adult daycare. Only services that are considered "medically necessary" for the treatment of a specific medical condition are covered. Medicare will pay for a maximum 100 days of nursing home care under Medicare Part A, but only if a three day or more hospital stay has preceded the nursing home stay. Additionally, the program will only pay as long as you are showing progress in your rehabilitation. The nursing care must be assisting you with your recovery and should lead to your return home. Once your condition has stabilized, Medicare benefits will stop – even if you are still ill or not yet completely healthy.

Medicare is not a program to cover long-term care needs, it is simply a health insurance program for those over age 65. While it does cover doctor visits and hospital services, it is not meant for long-term care expenses.

Medicaid: Spending Down to Eligibility

When Medicaid was created back in the 1960s, it was designed to provide healthcare for people with low income and few assets. For seniors, the Medicaid program offers both good news and bad news. The good news is that Medicaid was developed to cover long-term care costs for Americans of any age who need help paying for those services. Medicaid currently pays about 45% of the national total spent on long-term care, primarily for nursing home facilities (although in-home care is increasingly becoming available).

The bad news is that Medicaid is for people who are

basically destitute. It is a form of welfare and requires a means test. Therefore, to qualify for Medicaid, you must first spend nearly all of your savings before Medicaid will kick in. Probably not what you had in mind when you started your retirement.

 Qualifying for Medicaid – By the Numbers

Spending Down: Here's a partial list of the financial resources that may be at risk if you are trying to qualify for Medicaid benefits:

- Assets over $2,000

- Primary home equity greater than $500,000

- Most personal income, although there are rules to prevent total impoverishment of a healthy at-home spouse

- Retirement accounts, e.g. 401(k), IRA

- Cash value life insurance

- Vacation home, second vehicle

We mentioned that you would need to spend down your assets to qualify, but what impact would that have on your family? The financial burden could be devastating. Here is how the government decides if you qualify for the long-term care benefits of Medicaid. When you apply for benefits, Medicaid will do what is called a five-year "look back" of your financial statements to look for any asset transfers you may have given to your family or to others. If they find that you transferred or sold a personal asset, then that asset is considered "available" for your nursing care and will disqualify you from Medicaid for a certain period of time. They basically take the value of the asset and divide by the average cost per day of a local nursing home. This will determine the penalty period, or period of time when you will have to pay all of your nursing care expenses.

Here is an example: Let's say you gave $25,000 each to your two grandchildren to help them with the down payment on a home. You made this gift three years before you applied for Medicaid. Suppose also that the daily cost of a nursing home in your area is $150. Medicaid would divide the $50,000 total asset transfer by the $150 per day cost of care, which would equal about 333 days of care that the asset could have paid for. Therefore, in this case, you would have to wait almost a full year before Medicaid would start paying benefits!

Where is that money going to come from? Not the grandchildren – they have already spent the money. This money will have to come from your spouse or other family members. Think of the financial impact this will have on them!

To make matters worse, the penalty period now begins the day you apply for coverage, not the day the asset was transferred. This policy is a result of the 2006 Federal Deficit Reduction Act.

Medicaid looks at two things – your income and your assets. The look-back period applies to your assets. As far as income, just know that even if you do qualify for Medicaid, you will still need to contribute much of your current income – Social Security, pensions and annuities – to pay for your own care. Medicaid will only cover the difference. As a final kicker, in a process known as "estate recovery," Medicaid can recoup money spent on your care from your estate after your death.

Remember that Medicaid is a program that was established to help our poor have access to healthcare and retain some dignity in old age. It was never meant for those who want to remain at home or protect their assets to pass along to their loved ones. For most middle income and upper income people, Medicaid is a poor choice for long-term care. The financial impact on you and your spouse, and on your ability to pass your hard-earned assets to your family would be just too great.

Going It Alone or Spreading the Risk: Long-Term Care Insurance

If the government requires you to spend down your hard-earned assets before they pay for your long-term care, what other options do you have? There are basically two options moving forward: you can pay for long-term care out of your own assets or you can transfer the risk to an insurance company and they will pay for your care. Insurance involves pooling a small portion of your assets with a bunch of other people who, just like you, are trying to protect themselves from this same risk. Those who eventually need the assistance will the get the money. Those who do not need assistance will be rewarded with the peace of mind of knowing that if they had needed the care, the money would have been available to them. This "pooling" is accomplished by buying a long-term care policy. Each month or year, you pay a premium to the insurance company in exchange for an amount of coverage. Here is a look at your options.

The first option is to self-fund. Self-funding simply means that you will pay all of the expenses for your care with your personal savings and assets, at least until you spend down enough to qualify for Medicaid. This happens to be one of the most popular options, because if you have not made a plan for your long-term care, the government has established this plan for you. You may not like this plan, but it is the default option. But is it your best option? Let's step back and review your life so far. You probably have a home, a couple of cars, a 401(k), and maybe some type of brokerage or savings account. You may own some CDs, annuities and some life insurance. You are trying to build some wealth, but at the same time protect yourself from large-scale disasters. You probably have homeowner's insurance, automobile insurance, maybe some disability insurance. These are all prudent ways to handle risk. If a rock goes through a windshield, you could probably afford to replace the windshield. But if your car was totaled in an accident, you would be glad you had collision coverage.

However, at retirement, some of these protections disappear. You may lose the group life insurance and disability coverage you had at work. Your other term life policy might be too expensive to keep. Your income may change from a bimonthly paycheck to a monthly annuity and Social Security check. As we have discussed, your strategy will probably change from accumulating assets to taking income that will last a lifetime. If you think about it, nobody lives on principal – they live on income. You will get a check from Social Security every month and possibly a pension. But those checks really only help to cover basic expenses. It is the income you receive from your investments that generate the extra income you use to really enjoy your retirement.

But what if you developed a medical condition that required you to need long-term care? You would certainly start by using your current income, but as we discussed, given the costs involved that would not be enough. You would then have to start spending your investment principal. However, doing so will change the entire course of retirement for both you and your spouse. The retirement savings that was supposed to last a lifetime just got spent for a few years of long-term care.

The final answer? Well, you could take the chance that you might be one of the lucky ones who will not need long-term care. But the odds would be against you. About 70% of Americans will need some form of long-term care before they die. If you do not have a plan to pay for these costs, the results will be devastating. So why gamble? Even wealthy people are far better off using pennies today than paying dollars tomorrow. The final funding option is long-term care insurance (LTCi). Long-term care insurance works as a partner to your health insurance and Medicare since long-term care insurance does pay for custodial care. Your health insurance and Medicare cover acute care. Since each covers different types of services and care, a shortfall in one is likely to be covered by the other. According to the American Association for Long-Term Care Insurance, over 8 million Americans are covered by long-term care insurance.

Long-term care insurance pays for services across the spectrum of care options, including:

- Home care
- Adult daycare
- Assisted living facility/residential care facility
- Nursing facility
- Hospice care

LTCi addresses some of the limitations we discussed earlier. There is no hospital stay requirement and no income or asset test to pass for receiving benefits. The policyholder must simply meet the benefit triggers identified in the policy and satisfy the elimination or waiting period indicated on the policy to qualify for benefits. These can normally be found on the Schedule of Benefits page of the policy.

Long-term care insurance provides benefits for services needed by the person listed on the policy, but can help protect the entire family as well:

Financially – by allowing you to spend money on what you *want* to spend it on rather than what you *have* to spend it on. It can leave retirement and estate plans and strategies intact.

Emotionally – available resources, like the guidance of a care coordinator, can allow your family to be with you while you are receiving care rather than having to administer it. This can help you stay in your home longer.

There are many stories in the media today about long-term care and a variety of companies that offer policies. How do you sort through all of the information to find the best fit for you? When shopping for long-term care insurance:

- Start with the company. Look for high financial ratings and a history of integrity. You may not need this policy for 20 or 30 years, so you want the company to be as reliable as possible. Your peace of mind will depend on the financial strength and stability of your insurer.

- Look for a comprehensive insurance policy that offers a wide range of benefits, because everyone's needs are different at the time of a claim. Some features to consider are length of coverage (period of years or lifetime), home healthcare coverage, the daily benefit rate, and whether the payments are inflation-adjusted.

Why Buy Long-Term Care Insurance?

Consider these benefits when you have a long-term care policy:

- **Retaining independence and dignity.** As opposed to seniors who lose all control of their future when they go on Medicaid, seniors who have a long-term care policy retain significantly more control. They can decide to remain in their home or choose from the many assisted living facilities available. Medicaid may not allow you much choice of how you will be cared for. Not all nursing facilities accept Medicaid and you certainly will not have a private room.

- **Protecting the healthy spouse.** Married seniors

must consider how their long-term care will affect the other spouse. For those without coverage, a spouse may be forced to pay for a caregiver from savings and the financial burden may leave minimal remaining assets for the spouse.

- **Asset protection.** An unanticipated long-term care event can literally wipe out an entire life's work. Long-term care insurance helps protect your assets from the devastating costs of an expensive illness.

- **Removal of the care-giving burden from family members.** Instead of enduring the mental and physical stress providing care can cause, your family can spend their time enjoying your company.

- **Peace of mind.** If you are single or do not have any close relatives nearby, long-term care insurance can reassure you that your needs are going to be taken care of. Long-term care insurance can coordinate the care you may need as well as pay for it.

Flexibility: Percentage of Claims Paid For	
Home Care	43.0%
Assisted Living	30.5%
Nursing Home	25.7%

Source: American Association for Long-Term Care Insurance, 2008 LTCi Sourcebook

What Determines the Cost of a Long-Term Care Policy?

Long-term care insurance is not as expensive as many people believe, especially in comparison to the potential cost of not having it. Here is a simple exercise for those who think it is expensive. Go on a little field trip to any assisted living facility or nursing home and sit down with some of the families that are visiting. Ask them how things are going – financially, emotionally, and health-wise. You will change your opinion pretty quickly.

The actual cost of the insurance will depend on a number of factors:

- Your age and your spouse's age at time of application

- Your health

- The amount of benefit you choose

- How long you want the benefit to pay for your care (e.g., three or five years)

- Specific policy features you select

- Any discounts you may be eligible for

There are many ways to pay for your insurance – wages, investment income – but one of the most efficient ways is using a lifetime income annuity because of the mortality credits. Do not automatically go with the lowest premium when you are out shopping. Over the past 10 years, many companies that came out with low premiums have had to significantly raise those premiums. This situation means policyholders are now in their 70s or 80s, on fixed incomes, and having to pay higher premiums. The most important thing to shop for is the strength of the insurance company and their history in the long-term care market.

A Money-Back Guarantee on Long-Term Care Insurance?

Many people do not know about this provision in some long-term care insurance policies: if a policy holder never uses his long-term care benefit, the premiums can be reverted to his family. This refund comes in the form of a death benefit. It helps overcome the objection that some people have to long-term care insurance. That objection sounds like this: "I don't want to spend my money on something I don't think I'm going to need. If I don't need the coverage, I just wasted my money on unnecessary insurance premiums."

First of all, that objection could be used for homeowner's insurance, auto insurance, or any other type of insurance. However, some long-term care policies offer a "Premium Refund Rider." This rider guarantees that you will either use the coverage while you are alive, or your family will be refunded all of your premiums at your death. Ask your financial advisor or insurance agent if that option is available for you. The option will increase the premium, but many people, especially high net worth individuals and business owners, like it. If you have a C corporation, for example, all long-term care premiums are tax-deductible as well!

When Should You Purchase a Long-Term Care Policy?

The simple answer is: as soon as possible. You cannot just go out and buy a long-term care policy. You have to qualify for it based on your health. Do not wait until you get a serious illness. Besides, the premiums are lower the younger you are. Delaying will make the premiums increasingly expensive, and that is *if* you can even still get it. There are many people out there who would happily pay five or six times your premium if they could get the coverage. But, due to their poor health, they can no longer qualify.

Ages When People Apply	
Under 35	1%
35-44	6%
45-54	26%
55-64	50%
65-74	15%
75 or Older	2%

Source: American Association for Long-Term Care Insurance, 2008 LTCi Sourcebook

The Million Dollar Problem

Long-term care has been referred to as a "Million Dollar Problem" that requires a solution. With people living longer and costs expected to go up in the coming decades, long-term care costs could represent $1 million or more in future liability for you and your family. Why face this risk alone and jeopardize your retirement and your ability to pass your estate on to your loved ones? By making a small investment now in long-term care insurance, you can solve the million dollar problem.

Keep in mind that everyone has a plan for long-term care – if you do not think you have a plan, let me assure you that you do. Now you may not like the plan that has been set up for you but you do have a plan: pay until you run out of money, then become a ward of the state, most likely in a nursing home. My plan is simple: I want to stay in my home until the day I die. I will not have to go into a nursing home. The nurse has to come to me. And my favorite part – I get to pick the nurse! I have a long-term care policy with a home healthcare coverage – I get to stay in my home!

I will bet that is the plan that you would prefer as well. But as I said – you cannot just buy a long-term care insurance policy. You have to qualify for it with your health. You cannot wait until you have a serious medical condition or you are unable to take care of yourself without assistance. Today is the healthiest day of your life. Every day from here on we will all be just a little older and less healthy than the day before. The time to get your policy is today. Do not wait. Long-term care insurance should be purchased in your 40s or 50s. That way you will have a plan that allows you to control your care and provide a solution to the million dollar problem.

Long-Term Care Insurance: What Is Your Plan?

 Key Points from Chapter 7

1. No retirement plan is complete without a plan for long-term care.

2. The odds of you losing your home to fire are 3%, totaling your car, 18%; but needing long-term care before you die – 72%!

3. Long-term care provides help with the activities of daily living. These expenses are not covered by Medicare. For Medicaid to pay, you have to become destitute.

4. Long-term care is very expensive. It can also cause physical and emotional stress to family members who are giving the care.

5. A long-term care insurance policy gives the control back to you. You can stay in your home, utilize assisted living, adult daycare, or other options. Money is provided to modify your home to make it easier and safer to stay at home.

6. You cannot buy a long-term care policy – you have to QUALIFY for it. You qualify for it with your health.

Chapter 8

Estate Planning: How Will You Be Remembered?

Just like no retirement plan is complete without a plan for long-term care, no retirement plan is complete without an estate plan. I have witnessed firsthand many disasters suffered by the families of those who did not have an estate plan. If you think about it, I have already discussed a number of very simple ways to improve your estate plan.

In Chapter 3, we met the 83-year-old gentleman from Texas who simply wanted a guaranteed paycheck for the rest of his life. When he died, he wanted his wife to get that same check. When she died, he wanted his son to get that check, then his daughter-in-law, and, eventually, his granddaughter. He could use an annuity to achieve his goals. That annuity was a form of a very simple estate plan. It was not a complete plan by any means, but it was better than what many people have done. If you remember, there were two questions I always ask anyone who inquires me,

"What should I do with *my* money?" Those two questions are: "What do you want your money to do for you while you're alive?" (Which is really about setting up a financial plan); and, "What do you want your money to do for you when you die?" (Which is what estate planning is all about).

In Chapter 4, we met the 70-year-old grandfather who wanted to do something special for his granddaughter. I recommended a joint lifetime income annuity that paid him a check every time his granddaughter had a birthday. When he died, she continued to get that same check every birthday for the rest of her life (she would never forget her favorite grandpa!). Ultimately, when she died, her daughter got the $50,000 tax-free death benefit (she would never forget her great-grandpa, either). This approach is a form of estate planning as well. A big part of estate planning has to do with gifting strategies – how can you transfer your wealth in the most efficient manner possible?

If that sounds familiar, it is: we said those words back in Chapter 6 when we discussed life insurance – life insurance is a wealth transfer issue. Estate planning is all about wealth transfer. In that same chapter, we looked at how to utilize life insurance to create an estate worth two or three times more than what you would have left to your loved ones without it.

This book is loaded with simple ideas about estate planning. This chapter will round out my thinking on the subject. It is not a technical chapter going into exhaustive detail on extremely complicated estate planning strategies. It will be more of an overview of how to create an estate if you need one, and some ways to transfer an estate if you have one. The more money you have, the more complex your estate can be and the more help you need. A good estate plan is not a do-it-yourself project. A good estate planning attorney and financial professional are worth their weight in gold, and they can help you save far more in estate taxes and probate costs than you would ever pay them in fees.

Creating an Estate

Those of you who do not have a significant estate may be thinking, "This chapter has nothing to do with me. I can barely make it my own." Others of you may not have any family to leave anything to. Still others may really want to leave some money to loved ones, but just do not know how to do it. There is a vehicle that offers tremendous leverage and can actually create a very large estate with a small amount of money – money that can go to the surviving family, a long serving trusted employee, a favorite grandchild, or even a favorite charity. I am talking about life insurance. Life insurance is the only financial product that can literally create a multi-million dollar estate out of thin air. A person could make a single premium payment to a life insurance company and if a bus hits him later that afternoon, the family could receive a multi-million dollar death benefit.

History is filled with stories of people who have made a huge difference to their families, universities, churches, and other charities with large life insurance death benefits. If you have not built the estate that you had hoped while you were working; by using life insurance, it is not too late to create a financial legacy. History is filled with tragedies of families who were left with nothing, or even worse, left with huge debts, when a breadwinner died with no life insurance in force. Please do not be one of those people.

Estate Planning Objectives

"Thrift is a wonderful virtue, particularly in an ancestor."

– Mark Twain

Estate planning involves leaving your property to your loved ones and/or charitable causes after your death. You may even transfer some assets while you are still alive to take advantage of certain gift tax exemptions and to provide assistance when needed (e.g., your grandchildren's college tuition). The first step is to get a handle on what you own, which includes everything from real estate, stocks, mutual funds, retirement accounts, and bank accounts, to personal property such as cars, jewelry, or art. Second, you need to start thinking about who should get what assets and when; then you can consider the best planning approach to see that it happens.

Here is a simple exercise. Take a few minutes and just think about your death. If you were not here, who would it impact and how? What would happen if your paycheck or pension or Social Security check stopped? Who would do all of the things you do every day? Who would handle the financial affairs, mow the lawn, take care of the kids (or your parents)? Are there important people in your life for whom you want to do something special? Any favorite charities? Start today by putting a plan together to have your money do the things you want it to do when you die. You cannot take your money with you. It all stays here. What do you want that money to do? How do you want to be remembered? Think about these issues as we look at some basic estate planning documents and how they are used.

Estate Planning Documents

WILLS

Remember in the last chapter when I said, "Everyone has a plan for long-term care. If you think you don't have a plan, you're wrong. You do have a plan – you just won't like your plan"? The same can be said for estate planning! If you die without a will, you are said to have died intestate. Intestate means that you will have no input in how your estate is distributed by a probate court. The state will decide how your estate is divided and distributed. The intestate succession laws vary from state to state but have similar elements.

A will is the most basic estate planning document. You can have a simple will or a joint will (there are other types of wills as well, but simple and joint are the most common). A will typically includes:

a. A description of who you are (enough information to clearly identify that this is your last will and testament).

b. The names of your beneficiaries (can be both people and institutions) and enough information (addresses, dates of birth, etc.) that whoever is reading the will can clearly identify them.

c. The name of the person you are appointing as executor to manage your estate and make sure the assets get distributed to the beneficiaries (it is a good idea to appoint a secondary executor in case the first is unable to discharge the duties). You should also get the approval of the person you are appointing in advance.

d. Your directions for who will care for your children, your parents, or anyone else for whom you are legally responsible.

e. How you want your assets distributed when you die. You can make both specific bequests (e.g., I leave my diamond ring to my niece) and general bequests (I leave one-third of my estate to my son).

Although a will seems like a simple enough document and the internet is loaded with do-it-yourself will kits, this is too important a document to not have it prepared and reviewed by legal counsel. Wills can be disputed. The laws on what constitutes a valid will vary from state to state. Spend a few bucks more to make sure it is exactly the way you want it to be.

One final point about wills is that they provide for the distribution of assets that go through probate proceedings. Assets that pass outside of probate are not distributed according to your will.

TRUSTS

The most popular document for people who have significant assets is a trust. If you do not have much money, you may not need a trust. A simple will may suffice. I say "may" because there are many people who have simple estates who prefer to have a trust anyway because of the privacy it affords. A trust is a legal document to hold and manage your property and assets for your beneficiaries. You can transfer some or all of your assets into the trust. The trust will ensure that your assets will be managed and distributed according to your wishes after your death.

Just like a will, a trust has several components:

a. The person setting up the trust (often referred to as the trustor, settlor, or grantor).

b. The objective of the trust.

c. The type of trust.

d. The property or assets that are put into the trust (known as trust property).

e. The beneficiaries (the people or institutions that will receive some or all of the trust property or otherwise benefit from the trust).

f. The trustee (the person in charge of the trust).

g. The distribution rules – how often money will be paid out. For example, beneficiaries could receive income from the trust or they could have the ability to tap some or the entire principal for certain purposes.

A trust is not a do-it-yourself project. There are many different types of trusts – revocable, irrevocable, special needs, intentionally defective, marital, A-B trust, testamentary, QTIP, GRAT, GRUT, GRIT, CRAT, CRUT, etc. Entire books have been published that explain the details on each of these. Financial advisors and attorneys can go on and on about their favorite ones and why, and it is important to get advice from a qualified professional when setting up a trust.

Why set up a trust? Trusts have several important advantages that you should understand. These benefits include:

a. **Reducing or avoiding estate taxes.** By using gifting strategies and trusts like an irrevocable life insurance trust, millions of dollars of potential estate taxes can be avoided.

b. **Avoiding probate.** By keeping your assets and property out of your probate estate, you can skip many of the hassles, costs, and privacy concerns that are a part of the public probate process.

c. **Protecting your estate** (and your beneficiary's estate). A trust can protect assets from lawsuits, divorce, spendthrift relatives, and much more.

d. **Provide funding for grandchildren's education.** You can designate funds to be used for certain purposes.

e. **Leaving a legacy that is handled exactly the way you want.** You can literally "control from the grave." Assets are managed and distributed according to your instructions long after you are gone.

MEDICAL DOCUMENTS:
DEALING WITH INCAPACITY

In addition to distributing assets at death, a complete estate plan should also include documents in the event that you become incapacitated through illness and are unable to handle financial and medical decisions. There are two basic documents you should have in place: a durable power of attorney and healthcare proxy.

A durable power of attorney allows the person you designate to handle your financial affairs just as you would, including accessing bank accounts and paying bills. The power is "durable" in the sense that it continues in the event that you become incapacitated due to physical or mental illness. It is a good idea to have this document because otherwise your family would have to go to court to appoint a guardian or conservator, which can be expensive and time-consuming. The person you select should be responsible and trustworthy.

A healthcare proxy is similar to the durable power of attorney except that it allows the person named in the document to make medical care decisions in the event that you become incapacitated. These decisions pertain to treatment, tests, and medication, as well as life prolonging procedures. You can give specific instructions to the agent regarding certain treatments that must be followed (e.g., no feeding tubes), or you can give your agent more flexibility. This document can help to prevent conflicts among relatives over medical decisions and will help expedite your medical treatment.

TO PROBATE OR NOT TO PROBATE...

Probate is the process whereby a state court manages the distribution of your property to your beneficiaries. If you have a will, the court will follow your distribution plan. In the event that you do not have a will, the assets are distributed according to the laws of intestacy in your state. However, not all assets have to pass through probate. With proper planning, most assets can pass outside of probate. The advantages of avoiding probate include lower fees to lawyers and accountants, fewer delays in getting assets to beneficiaries, and keeping your distribution decisions private. There are several main techniques for avoiding probate. Trusts, discussed above, are one. However, there are two less complicated ways as well:

- **Joint ownership or joint tenancy:** Ownership will pass automatically to the surviving joint owner without going through probate. To use this technique, you would simply have to add another person to your real estate deed, bank account, or other assets.

- **Assets with named beneficiaries:** Ownership passes directly to the named beneficiary and transfer outside of probate. Examples of the types of assets with named beneficiaries include annuities, life insurance, retirement plans, IRAs, and bank accounts with payable-on-death designations.

By using these techniques, you can reduce or eliminate the need for probate and the associated fees and delays.

ESTATE AND GIFT TAXES

Under federal law, we pay taxes when we pass assets along to others. The gift tax applies for transfers made while you are alive, and the estate tax kicks in at your death. There are some significant exemptions from both gift and estate taxes. It is important to take these transfer taxes into consideration if you are thinking about giving your vacation home to your kids, paying your grandchild's college tuition, or planning the distribution of your estate.

To say that estate taxes have been a political football over the last 15 years would be an understatement. Estate planning professionals have been frustrated by the lack of continuity from Congress. It is extremely difficult to provide solid financial advice for the long term when the government keeps moving the goal posts. What is even worse is that clients are hesitant to plan for estate tax issues given the uncertainty.

Take a look at the estate tax table for the last 15 years! How could anyone feel comfortable about an estate plan? The estate tax applies to all assets that you own at death. Even if an asset avoids probate, it is still subject to the estate tax. The estate tax exemption is the amount of assets that pass tax-free before the estate tax kicks in. So if you were to pass away in 2014, you could pass along up to $5.34 million free from estate taxes to anyone other than a spouse. There is no estate tax on assets left to a surviving spouse.

In 2013 Congress changed it 5,250,000 and in 2014 to 5,340,000.

Year	Estate Tax Exemption	Top Estate Tax Rate
1997	$600,000	55%
1998	$625,000	55%
1999	$650,000	55%
2000	$675,000	55%
2001	$675,000	55%
2002	$1,000,000	50%
2003	$1,000,000	49%
2004	$1,500,000	48%
2005	$1,500,000	47%
2006	$2,000,000	46%
2007	$2,000,000	45%
2008	$2,000,000	45%
2009	$3,500,000	45%
2010	Unlimited	0%
2011	$5,000,000	35%
2012	$5,000,000	35%
2013	$5,250,000	40%
2014	$5,340,000	40%

Note the unlimited estate tax exemption for anyone who died in 2010. Due to a quirk in the law, the estate tax was eliminated for that one year. George Steinbrenner's heirs were big beneficiaries – they could inherit the New York Yankees and the rest of his financial empire free from estate taxes.

What can you do to reduce or eliminate the estate tax if you have assets beyond the exemption amount? I mentioned earlier that you could use trusts to help save on estate taxes. One of the most common techniques is to use an irrevocable life insurance trust or ILIT. If you currently own a life insurance policy, those death benefits will be income tax-free to your family. However, they will also count as part of your taxable estate. Since for many people a life insurance policy is one of their largest assets at death, this death benefit can cause them to go over the estate tax exemption amount – subjecting their family to estate taxes. A remedy would be to transfer ownership of this policy to an irrevocable life insurance trust. Once the ILIT owns the policy for three years, the death benefit is sheltered from estate taxes.

There are a couple of important caveats with this strategy. First, you need professional help here. There are complicated rules that must be followed which a qualified professional can help you navigate. Second, this is an irrevocable decision. Once you do this, you can never go back.

Very wealthy people often use ILITs as an estate planning tool. For example, if someone is worth $50 million, his or her family will likely have to pay tens of millions of dollars in estate taxes. If most of their worth is tied up in land or a business, they may have to sell the land or business at a fire sale price just to pay the taxes. History is filled with these tragedies. Go to www.EstateFailures.com to see some of these. This problem is easy to avoid. The person could buy enough life insurance to cover the estate tax obligation, and transfer the policy to an ILIT so it is not counted in their taxable estate. Upon his or her death, the life insurance proceeds pay all of the estate taxes and the family gets to keep the rest of the estate assets.

Life Insurance As a Wealth Transfer Technique

I have worked with a lot of wealthy people over the years. Whenever we get to the estate planning portion of the discussion, clients always have a tough time understanding why they should buy a big life insurance policy. I remember one case in particular. Ed was a very successful rancher in Colorado. He was worth around $15 million. We were recommending a $7 million life insurance policy to pay the estate taxes. Ed said, "I just don't want any life insurance! Heck, I'm loaded – I'm worth $15 million, why do I need life insurance? In fact, I'd have to say life insurance is the last thing I need. I think you boys are just trying to make a big commission."

This is a very common objection from wealthy people and I didn't even flinch. In fact, I smiled because I knew it was coming. I just leaned forward, looked Ed in the eyes, and said, "Ed, let me be the first to agree with you. You are worth a lot of money and you are correct – you don't need any life insurance. What you need is a way to transfer your wealth to your wife and kids in the most tax-efficient manner possible – would you agree with that?" Ed said, "I guess. And that is what I thought we were going to talk about before you started pushing this life insurance on me." Again, I just smiled and said, "Ed, if we could transfer your wealth with real estate, or stocks, or bonds, or CDs or Coca Cola cans, we would. But the tax code clearly favors one method, and that is life insurance. There is no more efficient way to transfer wealth to your heirs than life insurance. And Ed, that is not an opinion. That is a mathematical, scientific, and economic fact." I sat back, thinking I had done about as good a job as could be done. Ed was still unconvinced.

The agent, Bob Blach, who is a friend of mine, reached into his bag, and took out four plastic cows from a kid's farming set. He set the four plastic cows on the table. Bob said, "Ed, these are your cash cows. This one represents all of your land. This one represents all of your buildings. This one represents all of your equipment and this one represents all of your investments and bank accounts. Now, on the day you die, the IRS is going to come to the farm and butcher two of these cows." (At the time, the estate tax was about 50% after very low exemptions.) They will butcher those two cows and keep all of the meat. But it doesn't have to be that way. If we took some of the milk from each of the cows, we could take out a policy that will pay the IRS when you die, allowing all of your cash cows to go to your family. Ed, the choice is yours." I sat back in amazement. Ed's eyes lit up – he got it! He understood estate planning through the eyes of a 6-year-old with those toy cows! I learned a lot that day about storytelling and the power of simplicity. So, how do you want to be remembered?

A discussion of transfer taxes would not be complete without also mentioning the gift tax, which applies when you transfer assets to someone else during your lifetime. The gift tax is not as well known as the estate tax, but is equally important. The $5.34 million estate tax exemption for 2014 is actually unified with the gift tax exemption. What this means is that you can give away a total of $5.34 million tax-free during your life and at death. Any part of the $5.34 million exemption that you use to make gifts during your life will not be available at your death. For example, if you transferred a $500,000 vacation home to your kids in 2011 and you passed away in 2014, your estate tax exemption would be reduced to $4.84 million.

However, there are several exemptions to the gift tax that do not count towards the $5.34 million limit:

- **Annual exclusion:** You can give away up to $14,000 per recipient each year without any gift tax liability. You can make gifts to as many people as you want. For example, if you have three children and four grandchildren, you could give each of them up to $14,000 per year ($98,000 total) without worrying about the gift tax.

- **Education exclusion:** You can pay for someone's tuition without gift tax as long as you pay the educational institution directly. The education exclusion applies to tuition only; room and board or other expenses could be covered by the $14,000 annual exclusion.

- **Medical care exclusion:** You can pay for someone's

medical expenses as long as the money goes directly to the healthcare provider.

- **Spousal exclusion:** You can make unlimited gifts to your spouse as long as he or she is a U.S. citizen.

There are situations where it may make sense for tax purposes to transfer an asset during life rather than passing it on at death. Earlier in this section, I discussed transferring a life insurance policy to an ILIT to avoid estate taxes on the death benefit. Doing so would cause the value of the policy at the time of the transfer to count as a gift and could reduce the $5.34 million lifetime gift and estate tax exemption. However, the death benefit on a life insurance policy is much greater than the value of the policy while you are still alive, so the value of the gift to the ILIT is much less than the value of the policy at death.

These issues are complicated. Beyond the complexities, there is much uncertainty in the federal estate and gift tax law as we approach 2015. Twenty states plus the District of Columbia also have estate taxes that are on top of the federal tax liability (some states refer to it as an inheritance tax). The state tax exemptions are typically much less than the current $5.34 million federal exemption. So your family could end up in a situation where, without proper planning, your estate owes taxes to the state government even if it does not owe Uncle Sam. All the more reason to stay on top of this issue and consult with a qualified professional.

Estate Planning: How Will You Be Remembered?

 Key Points from Chapter 8

1. No retirement plan is complete without an estate plan.

2. You can create an estate with life insurance.

3. Estate planning is all about transferring your wealth and assets to your family or favorite charity in the most tax-efficient manner possible.

4. If you were to die today, who would be impacted? How? What can you do now to limit any financial problems caused by a premature death?

5. Wills, trusts, and medical documents may all play a role in how your estate is handled.

6. Estate and gift taxes can have a significant impact on your family. These taxes must be paid promptly and have forced many families to sell property and assets at fire sale prices. Plan now to mitigate any problems.

7. Wealthy, people always say "I don't need any life insurance." And they are right. However, they need a way to transfer that wealth to their family in the most tax-efficient way possible. That often leads right back to life insurance. Life insurance is the most tax-favored wealth transfer vehicle.

Chapter 9

And They Lived Happily Ever After

We started with the question "What Happened to Happily Ever After?" Things used to be so simple. People worked for 30 or 40 years – many times with the same company – and got a very comfortable pension to last them through their retirement. Because of shorter life expectancies, for many, retirement was a short period of time prior to death.

Fast forward to today – people are living longer, pensions are a faded memory of days gone by, markets are more volatile than ever, Social Security and Medicare are on shaky ground, and retirement has become a scary word. The greatest risk for pension fund managers is that they will not have enough money to fund future retirement benefits claims. You need to be similarly concerned about underfunding because you are responsible for managing your own retirement plan. We talked about the risks of inflation, deflation, living too long, and withdrawing too much. It is so important to understand the power of longevity risk. Longevity is not just a single risk in retirement – it is a *multiplier* of all of the other risks.

Think about it. If you only live five years in retirement, inflation really will not have much impact on your portfolio. It would not matter if you withdrew 10% per year since you would only be taking money out for five years. It would not make much difference if the market dropped 30%. None of the other risks would really matter if you died early in retirement. However, each additional year you live, the other risks grow exponentially! If you live to be 100, almost none of the formulas used for investment simulation would provide an effective solution. Inflation could devastate your fixed income or savings accounts. Withdraw even 0.5% too much money each year and you will run out. So longevity is not simply a risk – it is a risk that makes all of the other risks very real.

The Investment Two-Step: Guaranteed Income and Inflation Protection

The solution to this dilemma is a very simple: a two step process that is supported by math and science. Step one is to cover basic expenses with guaranteed lifetime income. First, you need to know how much money you need each month in retirement. Subtract out your Social Security and any pensions you may receive. The remaining shortfall needs to be covered by a lifetime income annuity. Because of the mortality credits, which provide additional benefits the longer you live, only a lifetime income annuity can optimize income over the indefinite period of a human life. Dr. Menahem Yaari proved this in the 1960s. If you do not use a lifetime income annuity, one of the following will be true: you will either spend too much and eventually run out of money; or you will spend too little and never live the retirement you dreamed about.

The second step is to optimize the portfolio for inflation. This approach will be difficult for some conservative investors. If you have saved money your whole life in CDs, bank accounts, or other conservative investments, it will be difficult to suddenly invest in oil, gas, gold, real estate, stocks, TIPS, and other inflation-sensitive investments. Yet that is exactly what I am saying to do with some of your money. Remember, if all of your expenses are covered by guaranteed income, you have already removed most of the risks in retirement. You have taken care of longevity risk since you get those checks for the rest of your life. The payments will never go down, so you have taken deflation, recession, and depression off the list. Since the returns from lifetime income annuities do not fluctuate (they have a zero standard deviation – see chart on next page), you have removed market risk from the equation.

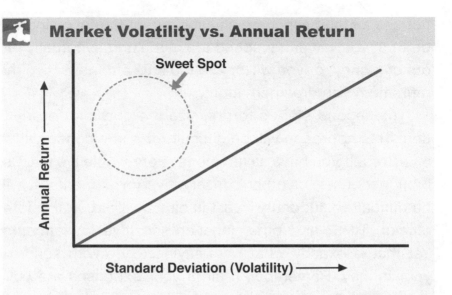

Market Volatility vs. Annual Return

Market volatility is measured by a mathematical concept called standard deviation. Generally, a higher standard deviation means greater volatility (and risk) but larger potential return. Our objective is to move your income-generating investments to the sweet spot of higher annual returns and less volatility.

What is the primary remaining risk? Inflation! So the optimization of the rest of your portfolio has to take inflation into account. The U.S. experienced high inflation during the 1970s, but then reverted to a long period of price stability. However, given recent government policies, it is possible we could see higher inflation rates in the future. Even relatively low inflation rates will erode your purchasing power over time and you will become steadily poorer if you do not plan for it. Investments such as cash, savings accounts, or CDs that return less than the inflation rate will not protect you from inflation risk. FDIC insurance will not protect you from inflation risk. Having comfort in how liquid your money is in a money market fund will not protect you from inflation risk. Knowing you have some cash in a safety deposit box will not protect you from inflation risk.

Consider some alternative investments, such as putting some gold in your safe deposit box. Get some additional income from oil, gas, or other commodities. Invest in some of the greatest growth companies in America – Apple, Microsoft, Exxon, Google, Walmart, McDonald's, and many others. These are the ways to help protect against inflation. Since your basic expenses are covered through guaranteed income (Social Security, pension, and lifetime income annuities), you can afford to put part of your portfolio in more volatile investments as a hedge against inflation.

The Other Big Threats: Death and Disability

What are some of the other risks in retirement that we discussed? An early death may not be a problem for you (since you are dead). However, it may be a huge financial problem for your spouse, your parents, or your children. Earlier, I asked you to imagine your death. Who would be affected and how? What did you want to have happen that now will not happen? We discussed the importance of life insurance – that it is actually a miracle product that produces exactly the right amount of money at exactly the right time.

We looked at all of the types of life insurance – term, whole life, universal life, index life, and variable life. The bottom line? The only policy that matters is the one that is in force when you die! Since death is a permanent problem, it is best solved with permanent life insurance.

A serious illness is another risk to both you and your family. Do you have a plan for long-term care (yes, you do, but is it a good plan)? Will you have to spend down your hard earned money on a nursing home until you qualify for government assistance? Will you be able to stay in your house instead of going into a nursing home? If you arrange your plan right, you will be able to stay in your home as long as you want without losing your life's savings – complete with your own nurse! If you want to move into assisted living – it will be your choice! No retirement plan is complete without a plan for long-term care!

The Ratings Game

Say you follow all of my advice. Are there other risks to retirement? The remaining risk is one that I have talked around but never specifically talked about – the credit risk of the insurance company itself. Many of the strategies I discussed involve insurance companies, and not all insurance companies are created equal. Ratings matter – they matter more today than ever! How can I say that after the rating companies let us all down in the 2008 market implosion? After S&P downgraded the credit rating of the greatest nation in the history of the world?

I can tell you that you have to remain very vigilant about the financial strength of whatever company or companies you use. Each year, read their annual report. Read the rating agencies' commentaries about them. The rating agencies are not perfect, but they do a tremendous amount of research and digging. The agencies are now subject to new rules and regulations regarding transparency and conflicts of interest. They will uncover significant risks and will write about them. Stick to the highest rated companies and you will be served well. It is not worth reaching down the credit spectrum for an extra 20 bucks a month.

Get Real: Real Problems, Real Solutions

I have shared some simple ways real people have solved real problems. Those over age 70 now know how to maximize their RMDs (Required Minimum Distributions) from IRAs or 401(k)s to allow themselves to live a fantastic retirement – the retirement they always said they were going to have. I shared my belief that you do not owe your kids a penny of your retirement savings. Leave them the house, the cars, life insurance, and any other left over money, but do not lower your lifestyle in retirement for them!

We talked about Roth IRAs and a recovery plan after a bear market. I responded to the usual objections to using lifetime income annuities – giving up control and liquidity, locking in low interest rates, that there are "better" ways to do this. Liquidity is not a one-time event – it is a lifetime event. A lifetime income annuity *increases* lifetime liquidity. By giving up control of a small portion of your savings, you gain control over many of the risks that you would not be able to control otherwise. I showed you how interest rates are responsible for only a small portion of the lifetime income annuity paycheck – especially at older ages. I showed you how to use laddering so that you are not putting your money into just one lifetime income annuity, but rather buying multiple annuities over time. As far as a "better" way of doing it, I guess I would challenge any financial advisor to show me a better way that he or she can support with hard data.

 ## Reverse Mortgage for Additional Liquidity – Buyer Beware

If you own a home, are 62 or older, and the property is your primary residence, you may qualify for a reverse mortgage. You probably have seen ads on television featuring celebrities like James Garner and Robert Wagner pushing these products. Basically, a reverse mortgage allows you to turn your home equity into cash in the form of monthly payments. In the event that you need some liquidity, a reverse mortgage could be useful. However, they can be expensive with high closing costs, and the terms can be complicated and confusing. It is important to get independent advice from a qualified attorney and financial advisor before entering into one of these arrangements.

Open-Minded Investors vs. Closed-Minded Advisors

I believe a few financial advisors may criticize my book as too heavily slanted towards insurance and insurance-based products like annuities. Why didn't I spend equal time discussing no-load mutual funds, managed money, ETFs (Exchange Traded Funds), options, futures, currencies, and whatever other investments are out there? Here is my answer: I support the use of *all* of these other products when appropriate.

I have used options in cases where I want to use some leverage on investments that I believe will appreciate. The real danger with options is that you not only have to be right – you have to be right at the right time. I have used mutual funds – both load and no-load. I like mutual funds for the simple reason that I believe the professionals can probably invest better than I can – even though I stay very connected to the markets. There are some great money managers out there and you should take advantage of the most talented ones. I also used ETFs in my investing strategies. ETFs are really just mutual funds that you can trade in real time – just like a stock or bond. Normal mutual funds have a daily settlement. You can buy or sell at the closing price. With an ETF, you can buy and sell throughout the day. As far as futures and currencies, these are generally not do-it-yourself projects. You can lose money very quickly if you do not know what you are doing.

The reason this book did not focus on those investments is because I do not think most retirees want the risk and volatility associated with many of these investments. They certainly are not appropriate to cover basic expenses. Basic expenses need to be covered by guaranteed income. If a product is used that does not contain mortality credits, the math and science will show that it is sub-optimal. Some people will say they can do better than a lifetime income annuity. The truth is that some will do better. However, many will do worse – and many of those will run out of money.

There are advisors out there recommending plans that have a 70% chance of success. If you were flying across the country and the airline told you they have a 70% chance of making it, only a 30% chance that they would crash – would you get on that plane? No way! Yet you should trust your retirement plan to an advisor who says you have a 70, 80, or even 90% chance of success? With a 90% likelihood of success, that still means that at least one out of 10 goes broke. If that person were you, you would not care that the other 90% were ok. And the truth is that if you ran out of money, many of the other 90% would likely be in trouble as well.

All of these other investments may certainly have a place in the inflation planning part of portfolio optimization. In fact, by covering basic expenses with guaranteed income, the rest of the portfolio is much more likely to succeed and you can actually justify taking more risk with it. If you want to learn more about those types of investments, check out some of the experts who have written books about them. The important thing is to keep an open mind, ask good questions, and use common sense when discussing and evaluating investment options.

Closing Thoughts...

We wrapped up the book with a look at estate planning. We looked at wills, trusts, gifting, and life insurance. The chapter was not intended to be a detailed look at all of the latest estate planning techniques. Again, there are experts in this area who write books and articles. Estate planning is not a do-it-yourself project either. You need to take advantage of the financial advisors and attorneys who specialize in this area. Estate planning is all about minimizing taxes to you and your family and maximizing your assets to do exactly what you would like them to do after you are gone.

I said at the beginning of the book that I wasn't going to give you my opinions – I was going to stick to math and science. I would encourage you to read the writings of Dr. Moshe Milevsky, Dr. David Babbel, and Dr. Menahem Yaari. These gentlemen are truly experts in the area of retirement income. You can find their works in many places on the internet.

In summary, retirement Is not about assets! Assets can be lost, stolen, swindled, sued, divorced or decimated by a market crash. No retirement is all about INCOME – and I would say Guaranteed Lifetime Income! It is also about reducing risks in retirement. So the optimal retirement would really follow these 4 simple steps:

1.   Cover your basic expenses with Guaranteed Lifetime Income – this reduces longevity risk (since it is a guaranteed paycheck for life), it reduces deflation risk (since you are getting a paycheck, if prices actually go down during a recession or depression, you are protected), it reduces market risk, withdrawal rate risk and order of returns risk. See you really take 5 key risks off the table when you cover your basic expenses with Guaranteed Lifetime Income.

2. Optimize the rest of your portfolio to protect you from Inflation. Long term, you must protect yourself from the ravages of inflation. Stocks, Real Estate and some Commodities have historically done a good job with inflation protection.

3. You MUST have a plan for Long Term Care. No retirement plan is complete without a plan for Long Term Care. It is the ONE thing most people forget about that can literally wipe out their portfolio.

4. The most efficient way to transfer wealth upon your death is to use permanent Life Insurance. Too many people use money to leave money. They have $200,000 in some "just in case account" that is meant to go to the kids. They could have taken $50,000 to buy a $200,000 policy for the kids and then used the other $150,000 for their OWN retirement. See it is all about using your resources in the most efficient way possible!

What I do know is this: if you follow the basic blueprint I have shared with you in this book, whether we have inflation, deflation, hyperinflation, or Great Depression, you will live a happy and successful retirement. You will not have the stress and frustrations of your neighbors. Just educate yourself on the basics and seek qualified advice when needed. You worked so hard for this time in your life. These are now the best years of your life – go and live them to their fullest!

Appendix: The Math and Science of Retirement Income

If you have ever heard me speak, you have no doubt heard me talk about the "math and science" of a proper retirement. The person I quote most often in my talks is Dr. Menahem Yaari. If you do some research on Dr. Yaari, you will find he had really set the economic world on fire with his analysis of consumer behavior and lifetime income annuities. In a 1965 article,[1] he put forth the theory that a retiree who wanted to maximize his income would put *all* of his money into a lifetime income annuity. According to Dr. Yaari, there was no alternative that could guarantee a more "optimal" solution. The reason has everything to do with mortality credits. The risk pool can pay more than a person trying to maximize income on their own. Now, I am not recommending full annuitization. Dr. Yaari assumed that the retiree would not consider passing on money to heirs.

The benefits of an annuity-heavy portfolio are reiterated, 40 years later, in a study called "Annuities and Individual Welfare."[2] While the authors give possible reasons for not fully annuitizing a portfolio, they prove that in most cases, significant investments in annuities were optimal. The low utilization rate of annuities by U.S. retirees was not rational and was "plausibly due to psychological or behavioral biases."

A Shift in Time

One of the modern day heroes of retirement income is a gentleman by the name of Moshe A. Milevsky. He has written many pieces on the importance of using annuities in retirement. In one of his articles,[3] he said that the way most people have taken money in retirement historically was by using a well-diversified portfolio of stocks, bonds, real estate, and the normal investment classes, then withdrawing a fixed amount from principal, dividends, and interest. However, this "do it yourself" strategy will likely fail if you live too long or continue to withdraw money during an extended bear market.

Milevsky went on to state in this paper, as many revered analysts have before and since, that very few people actually annuitize their wealth even though countless studies have shown that this is exactly what they should do. Where Milevsky's study really differs from the others is in its attempt to determine when and how much a person should invest in annuities. For those over age 70 or 75, the evidence is really overwhelming on the side of annuities. However, for those younger than age 70, Milevsky makes a case for delaying annuitization, that the internal "load" or cost of the contract may not outweigh the benefits of the mortality credits. I will say that this paper was written prior to the lost decade of the stock market from 2000-2010 and the increased volatility of recent years.

Milevsky also wrote a paper with Virginia R. Young,[4] which built on Milevsky's earlier paper, then made some amendments. First, it highlighted that the more risk-tolerant someone is, the more they may want to delay shifting to annuities. Conversely, the more conservative an investor is, the earlier they would want to annuitize. This paper also talks about variable immediate annuities, which I mention in Chapter 5. They are quite rare, but you should keep your eye on these. Because variable immediate annuities entitle you to market participation, it may not pay to delay investing in them. I will say, again, that this paper was written prior to all of this market volatility we have experienced in recent years.

The Emerging Consensus

George Bernard Shaw once said, "If you laid all the economists end to end, they still wouldn't reach a conclusion." David Babbel, a Professor of the Insurance and Risk Management Department and Finance Department at the University of Pennsylvania, proved that Shaw's time-honored quote no longer holds true when it comes to using annuities for a "substantial portion of retirement wealth." Economists from coast to coast now agree that annuities are the best way to go. "The list of economists who have discovered this includes some of the most prominent in the world, among whom are Nobel Prize winners," Babbel and Craig Merrill wrote in a 2007 piece.[5] The tremendous value that annuities provide in retirement seems to be an area where most economists agree.

Babbel and Merrill go on to say that you should start by covering 100% of your "minimum acceptable level of retirement income" with annuities. This approach provides the most cost-effective and practical way to provide for security in retirement. Even after covering these basic expenses, you will still need to put a significant amount of your remaining portfolio in annuities while still investing some in stocks, bonds, and money market funds. I would add to this slightly, because I believe extra attention needs to be paid in the optimization phase to inflation-protected investments like gold, silver, oil, and real estate. Like Milevsky, Babbel says that while they can certainly complement the portfolio, stocks and bonds are no substitutes for annuities.

A Small Price to Pay

For those of you who believe that annuities cost too much, Professors Babbel and Merrill have some food for thought. The market for annuities has become so competitive that the fees (called "loadings") are extremely low. When you compare the one-time 0%-5% internal "loading" with the 1%-2% annual fees charged by mutual funds and managed money or back-end charges, which can be as high as 8%, the lifetime income annuities compare very well. They also remind readers that lifetime income annuities offer guaranteed income for life – something that mutual funds or managed money cannot do.

When asked if it would not be cheaper to cut out the insurer and create a "homemade" strategy, Babbel and Merrill reply that it would be great if something like that existed, but it is a fantasy. They could not find people saying the same thing about life insurance. And why not? Because it takes an insurance company to group a large enough risk pool of literally thousands of people all paying premiums. These premiums fund the death benefits that go to the people who die prematurely. The exact concept, in reverse, is what insurance companies do with lifetime income annuities.

As far as giving up control of some of the funds, Babbel and Merrill argue that far from being a disadvantage, giving up some control for guaranteed income is actually a smart move. Many people get frail as they age; their judgment becomes impaired. Think of how many older people have been taken advantage of not only by strangers, but by their own families. They become vulnerable to pressure to help their children and others with their retirement funds. Many people have lost everything in cases like this. Annuities also reduce the risk that people will withdraw too much or overspend. Babbel and Merrill conclude: "Sometimes we pay a very high price for maintaining what we think is control."

In 2010, Scott DeMonte and Lawrence Petrone, CFA of the Financial Research Corporation of Boston (FRC), produced a white paper for New York Life. The title of the document is "Income Annuities Improve Portfolio Outcomes in Retirement." Here is a cogent quote from their white paper:

> Income Annuities offer features others can't – high cash flow, uncorrelated to market returns; retirement alpha in the form of mortality credits, which only life insurance companies can manufacture; longevity hedging and liquidity features.

That sounds to me like exactly what someone would be looking for in a retirement income vehicle.

A Class by Themselves

As far as optimizing retirement income and retirement security, DeMonte and Petrone emphasized that their analysis found that there was no other investment vehicle – *none* – that could match the income annuity for providing retirement security. No other investment vehicle was as efficient in creating retirement income from assets. They went on to say that no other investment could generate more income per dollar of capital than the income annuity, and that they "perfectly hedge longevity risk." Now, think about what they are saying – there is *no* other vehicle – *none* – in the market today that rivals the income annuity for providing income and peace of mind in retirement!

Many financial planners and brokers use age 90 as the maximum age for retirement income plan illustrations. I believe they do this because their plans will not hold up much beyond that. Even though most people do not think they will live to age 90, the facts are very different. Keep in mind that 33% of men, 44% of women, and 63% of married couples will have at least one of them live beyond age 90. Therefore, if you are married and you set up a financial plan that will last until age 90, that plan will fail 63% of the time.

DeMonte and Petrone also looked at using other sources of income instead of income annuities. Their focus was on successful outcomes. They found that because of the mortality credits paid from a lifetime income annuity and the guarantee of lifetime checks, longevity risk is taken off the table. This more often than not ensures a successful outcome using a lifetime income annuity.

Don't Retire Without One

Few financial advisors have made the transition from accumulation to distribution. They still use systematic withdrawals from diversified portfolios or bond ladders to provide income. These investment vehicles subject their clients to market risk, interest rate risk, withdrawal risk, order of return risk, and, most significantly, longevity risk. To those advisors, the FRC report says: "We have proven that even a well-constructed moderate portfolio is likely to fail over the long term if investors get aggressive with withdrawal rates as many will." What is aggressive? Today, a 4% or more withdrawal rate is considered to be aggressive.

DeMonte and Petrone go on to say that financial advisors have the obligation of ensuring that their clients have successful financial outcomes no matter the economic storms we face. High inflation, market downturns, and medical advances in longevity are all examples of these storms. My question is a simple one: if a financial advisor does not use a lifetime income annuity, then optimizes the rest of the portfolio with an eye on inflation, how can he do that? The answer is: he can't.

The FRC report adds that most investors do not understand the secret sauce of income annuities – namely the mortality credits (think of it as a new form of alpha or investment return). Only life insurance companies can manufacture mortality credits. It is these mortality credits that allow a lifetime income annuity to have such high guaranteed payouts. No other investment can do this. That simply means that you cannot use futures, options, hedge funds, or any other vehicle to do what the lifetime income annuities can do!

Here is something interesting: did you know that the life

insurance industry has a limited amount of mortality credits and therefore has a limited number of lifetime income annuities it can sell? This was news to me! I did not realize that the supply of income annuities is limited. Therefore, in 10 or 15 years, these products may be priced very differently than they are today.

As a demonstration of the significant income possibilities using a lifetime income annuity, the FRC report said, "Currently, income payout rates from AAA insurers for a 75 yr old male are at 8.9%, a 770 bps spread over the 1.2% 5 year Treasury."

DeMonte and Petrone also noted that this product is perfect for the baby boomers who will be retiring in record numbers. They are coming into retirement with damaged portfolios. The credit crisis, dot-com dot-bomb, housing bubble, and euro crisis have really done a number on them. They will be seeking guarantees and less risk, and will be drawn to the high guaranteed income offered by lifetime income annuities.

For people who tend to shop for the highest payout rate, the FRC report cautions that ratings for lifetime income annuities are even more important than ratings on bonds since you are tied to a life insurance company for the rest of your life. It would be a big mistake to go with a lower-rated insurance company to try to squeeze out an extra $15 a month. The financial strength of the insurance company should be paramount in the buying decision. As Babbel has noted in his studies, the financial strength of the insurer is very important. The website SeekingAlpha.com puts it this way: "There are no more guarantees, only guarantors."

The FRC report found the following about adding a lifetime income annuity to a diversified portfolio: The portfolios that did not contain an income annuity significantly under-performed the portfolios that had a lifetime income annuity. Look, there is a simple test that you can do to try to prove all of this research wrong. Take any diversified portfolio (it must have both stocks and bonds), remove some of the bonds, and replace them with a lifetime income annuity. You know what it will do to that portfolio? It will reduce the risk to the portfolio and increase the returns! Here is why: when you add a lifetime income annuity to a portfolio, it functions like an AAA bond (with a CCC yield and 0 standard deviation or vola-tility). Try it. See if you can prove me wrong.

I do not want this to be a technical, geeky book. But I have to provide enough evidence for you to feel comfortable with my recommendations. For those who want to do more research, there are websites you can go to for more technical information.

---

[1] Menahem Yaari. "Uncertain Lifetime, Life Insurance, and the Theory of the Consumer." *Review of Economic Studies*. 32.2 (1965): 137-50.

[2] T. Davidoff, J.R. Brown, & P.A. Diamond. "Annuities and Individual Welfare." *American Economic Review*. 95.5 (2005): 1573-90.

[3] Moshe A. Milevsky. "Optimal Asset Allocation Towards the End of the Life Cycle: To An-nuitize or Not to Annuitize?" *The Journal of Risk and Insurance*. 65.3 (1998): 401-26.

[4] M.A. Milevsky & V.R. Young. "Optimal Asset Allocation and the Real Option to Delay An-nuitization: It's Not Now-or-Never." Working Paper, York University (2002).

[5] D. Babbel & C. Merrill. "Investing Your Lump Sum at Retirement." The Wharton School, University of Pennsylvania (2007).

SOURCES BY CHAPTER

PREFACE

Mark Whitehouse, "Fed's Low Interest Rates Crack Retirees' Nest Eggs," *Wall Street Journal*, April 4, 2011, http://online.wsj.com/article/SB1000142405274870341060457621683094 1163492.html

CHAPTER 1

"S&P 500 pensions, OPEBs remain underfunded," *BenefitsPro*, May 26, 2011, http://www.benefitspro.com/2011/05/26/sp-500-pensions-opebs-remain-underfunded

"The Underfunding of State and Local Pension Plans," Congressional Budget Office, May 2011, http://www.cbo.gov/ftpdocs/120xx/doc12084/05-04-Pensions.pdf

"Weekly Spot Price – West Texas Intermediate Crude," U.S. Energy Information Agency, http://www.eia.gov/dnav/pet/hist/LeafHandler.ashx?n=pet&s=rwtc&f=w

Marcy Nicholson and Mihir Dalal, "Smucker hikes Folgers coffee 11 pct in fourth rise," *Reuters*, May 24, 2011, http://www.reuters.com/article/2011/05/24/jmsmucker-idUSL3E-7GO1RJ20110524

Stephanie Clifford and Catherine Rampell, "Food Inflation Kept Hidden in Tinier Bags," *New York Times*, March 28, 2011, http://www.nytimes.com/2011/03/29/business/29shrink.html?_r=1

"Medicare rates could eat up raise in Social Security," *Associated Press*, March 28, 2011, http://www.toledoblade.com/local/2011/03/28/Medicare-rates-could-eat-up-raise-in-Social-Security.html

Mark Sarney, "Distributional Effects of Price Indexing Social Security Benefits," U.S. Social Security Administration, November 2010, http://www.ssa.gov/policy/docs/policybriefs/pb2010-03.html

"2011 Annual Report of the Board of Trustees of the Federal Hospital Insurance Trust Fund and the Federal Supplementary Medical Insurance Trust Fund," Boards of Trustees for Medicare, May 13, 2011, https://www.cms.gov/reportstrustfunds/downloads/tr2011.pdf

Stanley Pignal, "Brussels to Press for Higher Retirement Ages," *Financial Times*, July 4, 2010, http://www.ft.com/cms/s/0/fe168510-87b0-11df-9f37-00144feabdc0.html

Richard Jackson, "China's Long March to Retirement Reform," *ChinaStakes*, October 26, 2009, http://www.chinastakes.com/2009/5/chinas-long-march-to-retirement-reform.html

Karen Hube, "Special Report - Retirement: With their steady income payments, annuities are suddenly hot," *Barron's*, June 20, 2011, http://online.barrons.com/article/SB500014240531119044720045763924016086611120.html

"Retirement Income – Ensuring Income Throughout Retirement Requires Difficult Choices," GAO Report to the Chairman, Special Committee on Aging, U.S. Senate, June 2011, http://www.gao.gov/new.items/d11400.pdf

CHAPTER 2

Ellen Schultz, "Rosy Assumptions Could Wreck Your Retirement," *Wall Street Journal*, June 18, 2011, http://online.wsj.com/article/SB10001424052702304453304576391734231318102.html

Suzanne Barlyn, "Live Very Very Long and Prosper," *Wall Street Journal*, June 27, 2011, http://finance.yahoo.com/focus-retirement/article/112977/live-very-very-long-prosper-wsj?mod=fidelity-buildingwealth&cat=fidelity_2010_building_wealth

Ralph Silberman, "Survey: MetLife Reports that Pre-Retirees Overestimate Retirement Moneys and Underestimate Retirement Length and Needs," *Aging Workforce News*, June 27, 2008, http://www.agingworkforcenews.com/2008_06_01_archive.html

Jonathan Clements, "How to Survive Retirement - Even if You're Short on Savings," *Wall Street Journal*, January 17, 2007, http://online.wsj.com/article/SB116899974081778389.html

Laura Shrestha, "Life Expectancy in the United States," Report for Congressional Research Service, August 16, 2006, http://aging.senate.gov/crs/aging1.pdf

Scott DeMonte and Lawrence Petrone, "Income Annuities Improve Portfolio Outcomes in Retirement," Financial Research Corporation report, 2010

John Mauldin, "Inflation and Deflation: Navigating the Curve in the Road," *Seeking Alpha*, April 11, 2011 (see comments), http://seekingalpha.com/article/262789-inflation-and-deflation-navigating-the-curve-in-the-road

Joe Morgan, "Buy tear gas stocks, Greece Police running out of gas pellets...," *Seeking Alpha*, posted on June 29, 2011, http://seekingalpha.com/user/764315/stocktalk/1839136

CHAPTER 3

Suzanne Barlyn, "Live Very Very Long and Prosper," *Wall Street Journal*, June 27, 2011, http://finance.yahoo.com/focus-retirement/article/112977/live-very-very-long-prosper-wsj?mod=fidelity-buildingwealth&cat=fidelity_2010_building_wealth

CHAPTER 4

John Bledsoe, *The Gospel of Roth: The Good News About Roth IRA Conversions and How They Can Make You Money*, LandMarc Press Inc., Hardcover edition (January 12, 2010)

CHAPTER 5

Bob Graham, "Variable annuity sales better than overall annuity numbers in 2010," *Insurance & Financial Advisor News*, February 16, 2011, http://ifawebnews.com/2011/02/16/variable-annuity-sales-better-than-overall-annuity-numbers-in-2010/

John Huggard, JD, CFP, *Investing with Variable Annuities: Fifty Reasons Why Variables Annuities May Be Better Long-Term Investments Than Mutual Funds*, Parker-Thompson Publishing, 1st edition (June 1, 2002)

E.S. Browning, "Exorcising Ghosts of Octobers Past," *Wall Street Journal*, October 15, 2007, http://online.wsj.com/article/SB119239926667758592.html

Carolyn T. Geer, "The great annuity rip-off," *Forbes*, February 9, 1998, http://www.forbes.com/forbes/1998/0209/6103106a.html

CHAPTER 6

Emily Flynn Vencat, "Narcissists in Neverland," *Newsweek*, October 15, 2007, http://www.thedailybeast.com/newsweek/2007/10/15/narcissists-in-neverland.html

Kimberly Lankford, "Life Insurance After 50," *Kiplinger's Personal Finance*, June 2011, http://www.kiplinger.com/magazine/archives/life-insurance-after-50.html

CHAPTER 7

The 2010 Sourcebook for Long-Term Care Insurance, American Association For Long-Term Care Insurance, data by Milliman Consulting (2010)

Medicare & You Handbook, Centers for Medicare & Medicaid Services (2011), http://www.medicare.gov/publications/pubs/pdf/10050.pdf

"Your Million Dollar Problem," *Guide to Long-Term Care* web site, 2011, http://www.guidetolongtermcare.com/milliondollarproblem.html

CHAPTER 8

Laura Saunders, "The State of the Estate Tax," *Wall Street Journal*, December 11, 2010, http://online.wsj.com/article/SB10001424052748704720804576009962752688894.html

Linda Koco, "Is Estate Planning Dead?" *InsuranceNewsNet Magazine*, February 2011

CHAPTER 9

Peter Tchir, "Sovereign Debt: Has Europe Finally Discovered Alchemy?" *Seeking Alpha*, July 21, 2011, http://seekingalpha.com/article/280939-sovereign-debt-has-europe-finally-discovered-alchemy

What Does The Media Say About Lifetime Income Annuities?

- *"Annuities ability to generate superior retirement income is conjured by pooling risk. The annuities transfer savings from people who don't need it (because they are dead) to those who do. This ability to match assets to future liabilities sends academic hearts aflutter. Economists who study the retirement market have long been sold on the merits of annuities and frustrated by consumers' aversion to them. U.S. vendors sold a piddling $6 billion worth of immediate fixed annuities last year. The 2008 figure will likely be around $10 Billion. This in a country with $2.7 trillion tucked away in 401k's."*

Scott Wooley
"Risk Free Retirement" *Forbes*
(May 25, 2009)

- *"Retirees in their mid to late sixties should consider replacing some or all of their bond funds with immediate fixed annuities that pay guaranteed monthly checks for the rest of the policyholder's life... Knowing you have this money coming in [from an immediate annuity] can also give you the confidence to invest the rest of your retirement savings more aggressively."*

  Steven T. Goldberg
  "The 25 Best Mutual Funds" *Kiplinger's Personal Finance* (May 2005)

- *"A better bet if you're ... worried about running out of savings might be to invest some of it in ... [an] immediate annuity and invest the rest more boldly."*

  Ira Carnahan
  "Do It Yourself Retirement" *Forbes* (June 6, 2005)

  Use the annuity for basic expenses and other investments to guard against inflation.

- *Annuities are "part of a diversified overall retirement plan. You can always use the other half or three quarters of your money to invest in a mix of bonds and stocks."*

  Paul J. Lim
  "Finding Income in Retirement" *U.S. News & World Report* (June 5, 2005)

  This suggests that one quarter to one half of your retirement portfolio should be used to purchase a lifetime income annuity.

- *"... income annuities can assure retirees of an income stream for life at a cost as much as 40% less than a traditional stock, bond and cash mix. What it means is that retirees who need a nest egg of, say, $1 million, can live the same lifestyle with as little as $600,000 in an income annuity."*

  Jeff Opdyke
  "The Case for Income Annuities" *The Wall Street Journal*
  (August 8, 2007)

Why is that? Because of the mortality credits and principal that is included in each check. (This article discussed the report done by Professor David Babbel of the University of Pennsylvania's Wharton Financial Institutions Center.)

- *"Many investors approaching retirement think they have no need for annuities. But the lifetime-income guarantees offered by these insurance-company products can add security to portfolios that are mostly composed of stock and bond mutual funds..."*

  Lavonne Kuykendall
  "Making the Case to Buy an Annuity" *The Wall Street Journal*
  (March 8, 2011)

- *The happiest people in retirement were those who had a stream of guaranteed paychecks for life. Some had pensions. The others purchased lifetime income annuities.*

  Jonathan Clements
  "The Secret to Happier Retirement" in WSJ.com (July 25, 2005)

Jonathan Clements looked at what the happiest people in retirement had in common. He listed seven common traits, including surrounding yourself with friends and neighbors who you get along with, thinking ahead, and getting a guaranteed stream of income.

- *Retirees would likely have to "work longer, save more and delay their Social Security Benefits until at least full retirement age."*

    "RETIREMENT INCOME, Ensuring Income throughout Retirement Requires Difficult Choices," Report to the Chairman, Special Committee on Aging, United States Senate, GAO-11-400, June 2011.

    This report concluded that Social Security is not enough to retire on. It went on to say that seniors should "convert some of their savings into an income annuity to cover necessary expenses."

- Curtis Cloke, another friend of mine, runs the Thrive Income Distribution System. He has compiled a very impressive library of other articles on his website. Go to www.thriveincome.com/related_articles.shtml.

Acknowledgments

This book has been 25 years in the making. Because of that, I have many people to thank. There are some groups of people who have had a lasting impact on me and on what I do. I believe there are only a few times in your entire life where you get to work with a superior team. Times when you really have fun going to work every day; times when you are surrounded by talented people and you all work better together than apart. I have been fortunate to experience that several times in my life.

Raised in a small town in Minnesota, I grew up with an interest in money. Maybe it was because we didn't have much – I'm really not sure. I would collect coins and spend hours sorting through them looking to fill the holes in my coin collection books. I would exchange these coins at the bank almost daily. As a young boy, I sold seeds door to door to earn spending money. Perhaps some of my very best business education came when I worked as a paperboy. I had two routes and delivered newspapers every day for years. Today, I cannot imagine allowing my 10- or 11-year-old children to go out by themselves every morning, in the dark, in -25 degree weather. But that is what I did – every day – rain or shine. I actually enjoyed delivering papers in the crisp, Minnesota air. The hard part of a paper route was that you also had to collect the money from the subscribers. So every two weeks, I had to go door to door again (this time in the evening) alone, to collect the money. It was amazing to hear all of the excuses people made as to why they couldn't pay the $2.50 they owed for the two weeks! I really learned a lot about people and selling in those formative years. I also learned that hard work pays off: I always had a new bicycle, the best hockey equipment, and almost anything else that I really wanted. I earned trips to see the Harlem Globetrotters, Minnesota Twins and Minnesota North Stars. I learned early that hard work and self-discipline yield incredible results – regardless of your age or station in life. I also learned how important giving to others is. I am a firm believer in giving 10% or more each year to help others that are less fortunate than I have been.

At my core, I am still a military officer. I attended college on an Army ROTC scholarship, spent 6 years on Active Duty in the Army, and another 16½ years in the Army Reserve. I retired in 2006 as a Lieutenant Colonel. Whenever I undergo tough situations or stress, my military background will come to the forefront. The army taught me discipline, selfless service, and mission accomplishment – on time, in time, and right the first time. It taught me to appreciate the simple things in life, which we ought to bask in each precious day. War should always be a last resort – never a first resort.

My toughest years in the Army were when I was in the 3rd Infantry Division in West Germany. It was right in the middle of the Cold War, and we had alerts in the middle of the night almost weekly. The times in my life when I was the coldest, the hungriest, and the most exhausted were those I spent in Germany.

Later, as a company commander in the 7th Infantry Division (Light) at Ft. Ord, California, I had my most enjoyable times. I had a company that could literally do anything it was called upon to do, and do it well. I had a team of lieutenants who were just superb. We got along great; we had fun, but we also had the highest standards in the division. Morale was exceptional and I loved going to work every day. I honed my leadership skills in that assignment. I learned how to set the vision, delegate, and then hold subordinates accountable. I found that 100 people working together can literally move mountains. One of my lieutenants, Mark Cincotta, has stayed a lifelong friend. I tried to recruit him when I was a MetLife manager, but he went on to build his own very successful career in the financial services industry.

In the Army Reserves, I was selected to command a battalion. I was selected as a major and was soon promoted to lieutenant colonel. Again, we had fun accomplishing each mission. Soldiers love to do their jobs well and be recognized for their achievements. I pinned many medals on my soldiers over the years. I would not be where I am without the great soldiers of the U.S. Army. Even in my civilian jobs, I am always kidded for my strict adherence to SOPs (Standard Operation Procedures, which are really the military's version of "best practices"). There are way too many to mention, but special shout-outs to General Perrin, COL Foster, COL Raynor, CW5 Raynor, CW4 Waddell, and LTC Barth.

When people ask me where I learned to speak as effectively as I do, I point to my military training. When you have to brief a general, you'd better have a full command of the subject you are briefing them on, or they will literally rip you to shreds right there in front of everyone. I have watched it happen to others many times. Before one of my briefings, I always ensured that I was well prepared – I knew the subject cold, I anticipated the questions, I even had a plan of how to answer something I didn't know. I also tried to have other subject matter experts present so I could introduce them to the general and solicit their knowledge on the subject as well.

Everyone has two or three people in their lives that have made all the difference in launching them to another level. Jack and Garry Kinder made a huge impact on my life. When I was hired to be an agent for MetLife, I just didn't feel the training was enough for me. However, there were some dusty VHS tapes in closet. The tapes were of the famous "Kinder Brothers." I watched those tapes over and over and over. I can still answer some of the objections word for word. I would not be where I am today without the Kinder Brothers – period.

Joe Jordan and Ted Kilkuskie were officers of MetLife. However, they weren't like any other "home office" people I had ever met before. They made meetings come to life. I learned how important language and words are. They had fun and were exceptionally creative in explaining new concepts. They made learning fun – I have since called this type of training "edutainment." I never missed a chance to see them in action. When I started speaking, it was Joe who said "Remember, Hegna: the bigger the audience, the bigger the show!" Joe was (and is) a showman extraordinaire. I wouldn't be where I am today without him. I would also like to thank Dennis Barghaan and Gary Olivero for the many great memories while we were on the Variable Products team. A number of my fellow MetLife agents went on to enjoy great success of their own: Wayne Kandas became the number one agent at MetLife; Sue Ritchie has a great long-term care insurance practice; Eric Feller and Mike Mazzella Jr. are running an independent brokerage operation; Todd Miller has a successful practice in the East Valley.

In 1996, I was recruited by Bob Meredith to join New York Life. Sy Sternberg, the new CEO, had agreed to provide product experts to support the New York Life field force as part of his "I owe you" agreement with the field. When Sy took over, morale in the field was low. In just a couple of years, he turned the entire thing around to create what is arguably the finest field force in the entire insurance industry. Bob Rock ran the annuity department along with his deputy, John Meyer. They created a very powerful team of product wholesalers who energized the field and saw production numbers skyrocket. Bob Meredith put together his "Dream Team" which included me, John O'Gara (who now leads all of the product wholesalers for New York Life), Alise Miller (who leads the investment and retirement wholesalers), Matt Vahl, Ray Lynch (retired), John O'Brien, Joe Watson (retired), Steve Sullivan, Chuck Staley, and Jim Robinson. We continued to hire the best and the brightest in the industry but that team was, I believe, the most productive team in company history. Ted Mathas was Sy's hand-picked replacement. Ted took the lifetime income annuity product off the shelf, shook the dust off it, and put in the resources necessary to really make it come to life. He saw the value in mortality credits when few others even knew what mortality credits were. He hired Chris Blunt, who is the Executive Vice President in charge of retirement security. Michael Gordon and Debbie Moy also played huge roles in the success of the Lifetime Income Annuity product. I would like to say a special thank you to all of my friends at New York Life. I spent 15 incredible years with these great agents, managers, and officers.

My big break happened in 2008. Former Million Dollar Round Table (MDRT) President and New York Life agent, Walton Rogers, recommended me to MDRT to be one of the speakers at the Boomertirement Roadshows that were sponsored by PREP (a combination of many different insurance industry associations). We did roadshows in Dallas, Chicago, Washington, D.C., New York, and Los Angeles. These were held right during the market meltdown in 2008. It seemed as though everyone was scared to death. Many financial advisors didn't know what to say to their clients. It seemed like a terrible time for nearly everyone.

And yet, there I stood on the stage, saying that our industry was "built for markets just like these! Our products – life insurance and annuities – were built for markets like these." I gave a message that was loud and clear and very positive: that we had the answers for our clients, not Wall Street. FinancialPlanning.com said this: "When New York Life (Vice) President Tom Hegna took the stage, he delivered a loud, boisterous presentation that served as a full-throated endorsement of the insurance business. He left to a standing ovation from the energized audience – an almost surreal moment of optimism for an industry that has been battered and bruised by mounting capital shortages and a series of ratings downgrades." The top industry leaders attended those meetings.

Phil Harriman, a past President of MDRT, really took me under his wing and made sure that every industry leader at those meetings met me. He helped get me in front of the right people and I got an invitation to speak on the main platform of the Top of the Table Meeting in Kauai in 2009! What a huge honor. From there, it was to the main platform of the MDRT Annual meeting in Vancouver. Understand that two to three thousand people are reviewed for just 18 main platform slots. To get one of these slots you have to be good, but also a little lucky – and your timing must be just right! Terry Headley, the incoming National Association of Insurance and Financial Advisors (NAIFA) President, then called me and asked me to be the opening speaker at the 2010 NAIFA annual meeting. Others who really went above and beyond in helping me were Jeff Taggart and Tom Currey (both past presidents of NAIFA), Julian Good and Jennifer Borislow (past and present presidents of MDRT, respectively), and Jim Tyrpak, President of the Society of Financial Services Professionals.

In addition to a tremendous professional network, I have also been fortunate to have the unending support of my parents, Dave and Fran Hegna of Fergus Falls, MN, and my sisters, Mary and Becky. I am so thankful for over 30 years of marriage with my wife, Laurie, and for our three sons Ryan (a successful entrepreneur in Tempe, AZ), Sean (an engineer for Eaton Corp.), and JJ (my 14-year-old athlete who is basically the identical twin of Ryan, although they are separated by 15 years).

JJ had a brain tumor six years ago and underwent seven hours of brain surgery. Brett Favre, Franco Harris, Lydell Mitchell, and John Runyan all visited JJ in the hospital, because the Super Bowl was in Phoenix the week of his surgery. We are all thrilled at the incredible work of Dr. Daniel

Lieberman – we got the whole JJ back!

Then there is my 12-year-old daughter Samantha - Sami is a dancer, an artist, and a voracious reader. (She was very excited about being mentioned in my book.)

As for helping me with the book, Paige Stover-Hague of Acanthus Publishing and her entire staff were fantastic. A special thanks to George Kasparian, who took my words and ideas and helped me bring them to life. His research was spot-on and he is a true professional. Other members of the Acanthus editorial team also contributed significantly to the project: Luke Messecar, Andrew Padgett, Eliza Rosenberry, Theresa Yannetty, Matt Angelosanto, Stephanie Mann, Gabrielle Corrado, Rodeline Prince, James Molinaro, Andrea Weidknecht, and Lois Hager. Tazuko Sugajima and Morgan Laliberte, also on the staff of Acanthus Publishing, contributed the cover design, internal layout, and graphs and charts. Carolyn Burgess gave me some great input on the long-term care chapter. I travelled the country with Carolyn over the years doing many joint meetings.

So, as I said, this book was really 25 years in the making – to be honest, I guess more like 50 years in the making. My entire life's experience went into the pages of this book. I hope you take at least a few good ideas to better your own financial life! Be on the lookout for my next book, which will be coming soon…

Tom Hegna

Fountain Hills, AZ
September 2011